Smart Family History

Fast track your family research

Geoff Swinfield

the national archives

First published in 2006 by
The National Archives
Kew, Richmond
Surrey, TW9 4DU, UK

www.nationalarchives.gov.uk

The National Archives (TNA) was formed when the Public Record
Office (PRO) and Historical Manuscripts Commission (HMC) combined in
April 2003.

A catalogue card for this book is available from the British Library.

ISBN 1 903365 80 5
978 1 903365 80 9

Typeset by Gem Graphics, Trenance, Cornwall
Cover designed by Penny Jones and Michael Morris
Printed by MPG Books, Bodmin, Cornwall

Contents

Introduction: Getting smarter   1

1   A start in life   13

2   Out of school   61

3   Settling down   77

4   The fighting man   111

5   Courts and criminals   135

6   A matter of status   161

7   Passing away   191

8   Exploring further   225

Useful addresses   234

Useful websites   242

Further reading   245

Index   246

Picture acknowledgements

Front and back cover: 'A Family Bicycle', 1948
© Hulton-Deutsch Collection/Corbis

p. 224: General Register Office for Scotland

All other images: The National Archives

Introduction:
Getting smarter

Researching your family history is an enjoyable and absorbing, often addictive, pastime. However, after you have researched the basic sources for family history, you might reach an impasse and believe, as many have done before you, that there is no solution to your problem.

The difficulty may relate to comparatively recent ancestors, from the last 100 years, whom you expected to find in the records of civil registration or in the Victorian census returns. Alternatively, the stumbling point could be information about ancestors in the 16th to 19th centuries, when you had hoped to find the relevant baptisms, marriages or burials in parish registers.

Why have you reached this barrier? Is there a solution? Lateral thinking can help you to plan a research strategy that gives you a realistic chance of making a breakthrough. Usually, you can work backwards in time, using family sources, indexes and records of registration, census returns, parish registers and probate records to find births, baptisms, marriages, deaths and burials for your more recent ancestors. This should enable you to make progress back into the late 18th or early 19th centuries. With perseverance and ensuring that the facts fit, it should be possible to produce a proven pedigree, where there are no apparent anomalies to cast doubt over the identity of a particular generation.

Family history research doesn't always happen like that. You may find one of the following, which indicates that you have the wrong person on your family tree:

- your ancestor's age at marriage does not agree with the date of birth;
- a person's place of birth is recorded consistently in censuses, but he was not born or baptized there;
- there are dramatic changes in a man's occupation or social status over short periods of time;
- an 'ancestor' dies before he was old enough to father his children.

At each step in the compilation of a family tree, it is necessary to accumulate sufficient circumstantial evidence to ensure that no error in identification has been made. It is foolish to add a forebear you are not sure about to the pedigree just because you want to find a link back into the 17th century! Ancestor hunting is not a race or a historical version of one-upmanship. It is more satisfying to have a good pedigree which can be traced, beyond reasonable doubt, back to 1765, rather than a work of fiction and invention which links back to Charlemagne or even Adam and Eve!

If you have a good candidate for your ancestor, whose birth or baptism and marriage have been found and documented, this is a strong case for adding another generation to the top of your roll of wallpaper or your software database programme. However, before inking in the link, check to ensure that the person did not die young – if there were two people with the same name in the same area, you need to distinguish between them by finding deaths (or other information) for both. Try and find out when he died. Otherwise, you may later discover that he died too early to be an ancestor.

It is also essential to ensure that your candidate did not marry someone else or have children in a nearby parish, contradicting your assumption that he was living and producing offspring by his documented spouse. There may have been two men with the same name in the same area who married two different women.

If you find only one candidate, so be it. As long as the appropriate checks are made, that person will probably stand up to scrutiny. Problems in tracing ancestry usually occur when there are no suitable candidates in the immediate vicinity of where the family is last known to have lived or, alternatively, there are several good candidates in the same area. The amount of checking required depends on how common the combination of forename and surname is in that area.

If you are looking for a John Smith, take great care before accepting any candidate. If your ancestor's surname is rare, by definition there will be far fewer choices, although it is not unusual for cousins to share the same name. If the surname is common, perhaps the same unusual forename will be found in consecutive generations, allowing a naming pattern to steer you towards one alternative rather than another.

Try broadening the scope of the research into other sources. Can you find any other documentation which will give additional clues or vital evidence to prove conclusively your ancestor's identity? To do this, define what you need to find and which sources are likely to record the life of your ancestor – for example, if you know that your ancestor was in the Army, you can use his service records. This will depend on the time period, the person's occupation and the geographical area where the family lived.

Each century has its own particular records. You should select those that are the most likely to provide the information you want and which are relevant to the time when your ancestor lived. For instance, civil registration and census records do not exist before the 19th century, and the heralds' visitation pedigrees date from the 16th and 17th centuries only.

Similarly, many records are specific to a particular social class. Poor Law records can often provide an insight into the movement of the working classes in their search for work or residence. Inquisitions post mortem document the passage of wealth from one tenant in chief (someone who holds property directly from the Crown and therefore very high up the social scale) to his heir. Once you have decided what sources you should look at, find out where these records are deposited and whether they are indexed to allow easier access.

Also study the county or area where the ancestral family lived. A thorough knowledge of the neighbourhood will suggest travel routes that your ancestor might have taken for permanent or seasonal migration – the bane of any family historian! Distance and direction is limited by geographical features, such as mountains or hills, but is enhanced by roads, rivers and access to transport. A topographical map of the area will suggest the main routes that your ancestors could have followed.

One of the main meeting places for courtship and betrothal was the market or fair. Potential spouses, or indeed those who engaged in extra-marital liaisons, would travel to such centres of trade from anywhere in the area. The homes of partners who came together to produce the next generation could have been in opposite directions from the market town. Before the advent of public transport, the distance they might have travelled to meet would depend on whether they had to walk there, could hitch a lift or had their own horse and cart.

Labourers in their search for work would move frequently, but over small distances. Tenants or owners of land would be unlikely to move very far from the source of their livelihood and security. Professional men and tradesmen, with trans-ferable skills and no ties, could move consider-able distances to find a position to enhance their prospects. Very mobile people included soldiers, sailors, coastguards, excise men, canal men and, of course, their families. Many people moved considerable distances from their place of birth when they went into service, took up an appren-ticeship or joined a branch of the armed or government services. Women tended to move away from home when they married. Female servants often worked a considerable distance from home in the 19th century. In genealogy, we know where a member of a family ended up. Our task and goal is to learn where he or she came from.

There are many ways of tackling such a problem. The internet is a good research tool and some frequently used sources now have good online indexes. These can speed up access and provide new clues. But not all the important family history sources can be accessed through the web – it will not solve all genealogical problems.

In any case, some people don't like using a computer and others prefer to do their research in the old-fashioned way. Indeed, there is no substitute for returning to original sources and good techniques of investigation, and sometimes there is no choice when the most sensible source remains uncatalogued or unindexed.

Try reading the genealogical press for new ideas. Magazines such as *Your Family Tree*, *Family History Monthly*, *Ancestors*, *Practical Family History and Family Tree Magazine* – all available from your local newsagent – include practical tips on finding new sources, indexes and techniques.

Where there is a publication that deals with a source in depth, read it. Learn about it and the best way to use it. Also make use of the very informative Research Guides of the National Archives and the Family Records Centre. These can be downloaded free of charge from *www.nationalarchives.gov.uk/gettingstarted* and *www.familyrecords.gov.uk/frc/research/research main.htm.*

Join your local family history society or the one where your ancestors lived. There are also special interest societies, such as the Romany and Traveller Family History Society, the Anglo-German Family History Society and many others. Explore the publications that the society of your choice has produced. All societies are coordinated through the Federation of Family History Societies, *www.ffhs.org.uk.*

Some sources will require you to spend hours of research in a record office, sorting through dusty original documents that have not seen the light of day for years. For many people, that is the appeal of family history. Some sources and publications that you need to use may only be available in a large repository or library. Many can be found only in the London area. If you live a long way from the capital, call upon the inter-library loan system to access some of the published material you need. You may eventually have to plan an extended research trip to examine those sources and indexes that are not available elsewhere or in any other format.

You may be able to order copies of the documents, books or sources that you need through the Church of Jesus Christ of Latter-day Saints and their Family History Centres worldwide. Online cataloguing, such as Access to Archives (A2A), may enable you to identify individual documents so that that you can order copies from a record office.

This book aims to provide you with the new ideas and strategies you will need when you have reached an impasse. Of course, there are many excellent guides to genealogical research but they generally deal with the sources and records in the order in which they are best used, assuming no problems are encountered. That is rarely the case!

There are many different ways that even the basic sources can be used in research. This book follows on from the companion volume, *Easy Family History* by David Annal, but looks at research problems from a different perspective. It focuses on how to shortcut searches using tricks of the trade: how to find a good candidate for your ancestor; how to make best use of sources,

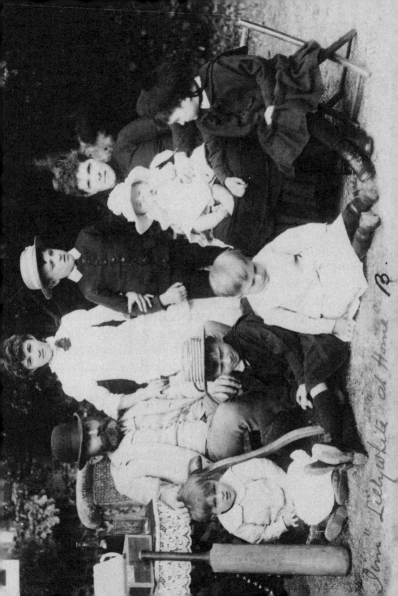

"Jean Lillywhite" at Home

such as calendars and indexes; how to localize the most likely place of origin; where to look for other untried sources.

This book has been structured so that you can follow each stage of your ancestor's life from birth, through marriage and work, to death. At each stage there are sources you can research and shortcuts you can make to fast track the process. New clues may be found from a missing marriage certificate, the birth of another child or a will. Learning about someone's career can shed light on where they came from and why they moved over 100 miles to settle in a new town or parish. By adopting a holistic approach to the lives of our ancestors, the answers to your research questions may become clearer. If just one idea works for you, then the book has been a success.

Chapter 1

A start in life

- Birth indexes and certificates
- Spelling problems
- Name change
- Indexes away from the Family Records Centre
- Using the internet
- Births outside England and Wales
- Adoption
- Identifying the right birth
- Baptismal records
- Church of England
- Dade registers
- Access to registers
- Copies of records
- Protestant nonconformists
- Catholics, Quakers and Jews
- Finding aids and indexes
- Ripple method
- Bastardy

The prime source of genealogical information is the record of a person's birth or baptism. Such records normally show the names of both parents, or in the case of an illegitimate child usually just the name of the mother. This is the main building block for a family tree since these entries give the names of the previous generation.

To learn where the birth or baptism of an ancestor may have been recorded, you need to know where the individual, or one of their relatives, believed that they originated. That information may be found in family papers or memorabilia. Vital clues can be discovered in service records and birthday books, or may be included in a Family Bible or letters.

In the absence of personal clues, you have to look for the information in a documentary source in the public domain. This may be a service record (*see* Chapter 4), a school, college or university alumni list or register (Chapter 2), or a professional source such as entry into a guild or profession (Chapter 6). Any source that records the life or career of a person can potentially provide evidence of age or place of origin, as it usually records the date and place of birth.

The main 19th-century source of such information is the census record. For England, Wales and Scotland, records that include names are available from 1841 to 1901. For those born out-side the country of residence, only the country of origin may be shown, with no statement of a particular parish of birth. Only the 1901 and 1911 census records survive in a complete form for Ireland, and these simply show the county of birth for those who were born within Ireland.

Fortunately, most of the censuses for Eng-land, Wales and Scotland have been indexed by name. You no longer have to search page by page through the original returns until at last you find the person you have been seeking for so long, recorded in the enumerator's hand. Today we use, and rely on, computerized indexes. Remember that no index is foolproof. If you do not find the entry you seek, go back and search the original returns using addresses obtained from other sources.

It may be difficult, if not impossible, to find people using known addresses. Your ancestors and their family may have been very mobile because of their trade or profession. There may have been a period in their life when they went into service or married, or perhaps they just chose to move frequently to avoid the rent man. In this case, the census indexes may be the only way of finding them (*see* Chapter 3).

When the family or individual is found, you have an invaluable statement of where and when that person believed they had been born. If the recorded place of birth is accurate, this can lead immediately to the next step, a birth registration or a baptismal entry in a church or nonconformist register. If the birthplace is inaccurate, this can set you off on a research trail to try and discover why the person did not appear to know where he or she had been born, or why they might have given false information. Such are the joys of searching for our ancestors!

Birth indexes and certificates

From 1 July 1837, all births registered in England and Wales should have been recorded by registrars and copied to the Registrar General. The quarterly indexes to 1983 and the annual indexes to the latest year that has been centrally compiled are available for research at the Family Records Centre. These are used to find and order copies of certificates. The indexes can be used in more inventive ways too.

For instance, from the September quarter of 1911, the mother's previous surname, as recorded at the birth registration, is included in the indexes. If that name is known, the correct 'John

Smith' can be selected from among all the other children of that name who were registered in that quarter. This very useful addition also allows the mother's maiden name or previous surname to be used as a search tool to find all her children, and from this you can compile family groups without having to obtain copies of birth certificates for each child.

The national birth indexes are far from perfect. They show only the district in which the birth was recorded and the volume and page number so that the entry can be ordered. Unfortunately, from the September quarter of 1910 to the end of 1965, the registered names are abbreviated to a first name and only initials for second, third and subsequent given names. How can you identify your John Jeremiah Smith among all those with much more common names like John James and John Joseph? All are indexed as John J. Smith.

Before mid-1911, in the case of a common combination of forename and surname, each quarter of the indexes will include several, if not tens of, possible entries for an ancestor. The most likely candidates can only be selected on the basis of the registration district or area where it is most probable that the ancestor was born. It is quite possible that a birth may have taken place many miles away from where the man or woman later married, lived or died. Some of the candidates may be eliminated as they appear as infants or young children in the death indexes, dying in that district. A very common name may make the search for the birth certificate impossible without further information from another source.

It should also be remembered that until 1874, registration of births was not strictly compulsory. Thus, especially in the very early years, many births were not recorded and are absent from the indexes. Some are missing from the indexes because they did not reach the central register in the first place. No matter how hard the reference entry is sought, it will not be found. If so, another source of parentage must be looked for, such as the child's baptismal record.

Spelling problems

Another common problem when searching the indexes is the variety of spellings that can occur. The mishearing of the original surname at registration may have caused variation from the expected spelling. This may have been a result of the unfamiliar accent of the informant, or the person trying to provide the name of the child may have had a cold, been intoxicated or even had a speech impediment. Many informants, who could not read or write, could not correct what was recorded. The registrar had to make the best interpretation of what he thought he heard. When you are searching for a missing entry, you must be inventive in guessing how a name may have been misinterpreted and hence recorded. The most difficult problem to solve is if the first or second letter is wrong. It should be remembered that the exact spelling of many surnames was not fixed until the late 19th century. It is no good being pedantic in believing that your surname was always spelt with an 'e' on the end.

Other changes in the spelling of surnames occurred between registration and the compilation of the national indexes now used at the Family Records Centre. As copying processes were needed to send a version of each entry from the local registrar to the Registrar General, these provided the opportunity for errors to be perpetrated and changes to be made to what had originally been registered. Once there, the handwriting had to be read and interpreted in order to put the name of the child in the correct place in the index. In the case of bad handwriting this may not have happened, making future searching even more difficult.

Name change

Some individuals changed their names during their lifetime – for example, women altered their surnames at marriage. It may be that the person you are searching for had been married before. If so, she may have married under a name that was not her maiden name. When her children were registered, she may have used her previous married name as though it was her original birth surname. Not all our female ancestors told their husbands about an earlier spouse.

People changed their names to go into enter-tainment, to join the armed services or to avoid the law. Others just wanted a new name. This may have been assumed or may have been formally changed by Deed Poll or advertisement, such as those that can be seen in the *London Gazette*. If so, the task of locating the birth, marriage or death of your person can be very difficult, if not impossible. Many forebears hid their tracks very effectively.

Some of our ancestors were registered with a name at birth but, for some reason, chose not to use it in the same way later in life. It is not un-usual for the first given name to be dropped when a person marries or is recorded in official documents. They probably disliked the name that their parents had chosen and decided not to use it. The order of their original registered names may have been switched around in all subsequent records. Others assumed nicknames, John always being known as Jack. The search for the true name of Minnie or Ellie can be a minefield! Other forenames were added after registration, such as at baptism or confirmation, and those names do not appear in the birth indexes.

In some instances, the name of the child was not decided by the time the parents registered their son or daughter. When you are searching, it is always worth looking at the end of each surname section in the quarterly index volume to see if any child was recorded simply as 'male' or 'female' in the right district. Most of these died very young but some did survive and were formally named later. Again, check the death indexes to see if that child died young.

The inadequacies of the indexes and changes of name can make searches and the identification of the required entry very difficult. This is especially true when dealing with common surnames.

Indexes away from the Family Records Centre

To avoid searching systematically through the original volumes of the national indexes at the

Family Records Centre, you may be able to try elsewhere first. There are a number of other ways in which the indexes can be searched which do not require a visit to Islington. If it is physically impossible to visit the Family Records Centre, these will be invaluable.

Many record offices and larger local libraries have microfiche (or even microfilm) copies of sections of the national indexes. You can discover which libraries hold the indexes through *www.familia.org.uk*.

Using the internet

Pay-for-view access to the images of the indexes from 1837 to the present can be achieved through *www.1837online.com* or *www.bmdindex.co.uk*. Both allow you to work from the comfort of home, making listings or seeking the required entry from which the certified copy can be ordered. In each case, you pay to see each page of the indexes where the name might appear.

The site *www.familyrelatives.org* provides a pay-for-view method of searching the indexes. You can request a listing of all possible entries for a particular birth (marriage or death) in a given time period. This is displayed on screen. Searches can be done from 1866 to 1920 at present. The list can be sorted chronologically or by district. If the name is very common, the search can be limited to a geographical area. From the September quarter of 1911, when the mother's maiden surname is shown, this can be used as a search tool to select possible siblings. This site provides a very valuable finding aid and labour saver.

Online searchable indexes are currently being produced from the records of individual counties or registration districts. Links to these can be found through *www.ukbmd.org.uk*. As these are indexes to the original birth registrations, held locally, they may be more complete and accurate than the national index at the Family Records Centre. You may find entries for registrations that did not reach the Registrar General. A copy of any relevant certificate can be ordered online.

A cumulative, though incomplete, version of the indexes can be accessed through *http://freebmd.rootsweb.com*. Changing almost daily, it will eventually be complete from the start of the system in 1837. At present, the index is reasonably complete to the early 20th century. The current coverage is shown on graphs on the site. In some periods, nearly all of the indexed entries are included. The images of the original volumes, from which the index is being compiled, are also available online.

FreeBMD allows you to request all references currently in the index to a given person in a selected time period. If the name is very common, the search can be limited to one or more registration districts or counties. The index is particularly useful for spotting possible siblings, especially if they had a distinctive first or second given name, which may have been a surname from a previous generation.

While using this version of the indexes, make use of the wildcard search. This can be used to find references that are to be found under a variant spelling. You will not have to search through each spelling that you can think of or, indeed, those that have yet to come to mind. If you cannot find the birth of a child whose name should be John Phillips, do the search just asking for any surname which begins with 'Phil'. You may find him registered as Philps. Indeed, it is even possible to search by forename alone if this is reasonably uncommon.

Birth outside England and Wales

You must also remember that there are other places where the birth could have been recorded.

If the father was in one of the armed services, perhaps his children were born wherever he was stationed. This usually relates to those in the Army, as soldiers were more likely to have taken their families with them when they were sent abroad. This was more difficult for sailors. For some other reason, your ancestor may have been overseas at the time of his child's birth. If so, the registration may be found in the separate indexes to the Statutory Returns. These include births of the children of servicemen that took place in the British Isles too.

The separate index volumes are in the General Register Office section of the Family Records Centre on the ground floor. They are also included in the microfiche version and can be searched in any library that holds a copy of the indexes in that format, and may be accessed on the *www. 1837online.com* database. Apart from some Army births, there are few, if any, entries for births in colonies or Commonwealth countries.

If the parents of the child were on the Indian sub-continent or in parts of Asia and Africa, the father being in the services or working as a tradesman, government official or civil servant, the child may be located in the ecclesiastical returns held at the Oriental and India Office

Smart data: Records of births abroad

Army regimental registers and supplement volume	1761–1924
Army chaplains' returns	1796–1965
Consular births	1849–1965
UK High Commission births	prior to 1981
Ionian islands	1818–64
Marine births	1837–1965
Air births	1947–65
Births abroad (includes all the types of record listed above)	1966 onwards

section on the 3rd floor of the British Library. This is part of the Asia, Pacific and Africa Collections. Births were not registered but baptismal records were returned to England. Indexed separately by each of the Presidencies of India (Bengal, Madras and Bombay), these date from as early as 1698 to Independence in 1947.

Non-statutory returns of birth and baptism were returned from those serving on British and foreign ships, from British subjects abroad and from British nationals who were living in colonies and Commonwealth countries under British control. The deposit of such records was voluntary. They are far from complete and, of course, only contain a selection of births of British children which took place abroad. They were transferred to the Public Record Office in 1977 and are now available on microfilm at the National Archives or on the first floor of the Family Record Centre in RG 32 to RG 36. They are indexed for births in RG 43/1 and 2 and 10–14 and date from as early as 1627.

Sometimes this material duplicates that in the Statutory Returns in the Miscellaneous Section of the General Register Office section at the Family Records Centre. See *Tracing Your Ancestors in the Public Record Office* by Amanda Bevan for a detailed listing of the overseas material held in Registrar General and Foreign Office series at the National Archives.

If the required birth or baptism is not found in these records, the birth may have taken place elsewhere in the British Isles or in the rest of the world and have been recorded locally.

The records of civil registration for Scotland date from 1855; those for Ireland from 1864; Northern Ireland from 1922; and the Isle of Man from 1849. The Channel Islands have separate records for each island and these begin as early as 1840. You must consider the possibility that the birth was recorded in one of those other places. For those who lived close to the border between England and Scotland, you should not be surprised if their records are to be found in Edinburgh.

A further source of a birth or baptism for an ancestor is the so-called International Memoranda held at Guildhall Library. Returns of chaplains, embassies, missions and some British factories were sent to the Bishop of London from 1816 to 1924. Such records are indexed on the open shelves in MS 10926C and the original returns are in MS 10926. Later deposits for 1921 to 1969 are for the Diocese of Gibraltar (though surprisingly not for Gibraltar itself) in MS 23607. A guide to the registers deposited at Guildhall Library and elsewhere, especially at the National Archives, can be found in *The British Overseas: A Guide to Records of Their Baptisms, Births, Marriages, Deaths and Burials Available in the United Kingdom* by Geoffrey Yeo, revised by Philippa Smith.

Many of our ancestors or relatives went to other parts of the world in the 19th century for various reasons. Whether it was to seek gold in California or whether they were granted a free passage to Australia for seven years 'at Her Majesty's pleasure', the records of the births of their children may be recorded by their state or country of temporary residence. Each had its own system of registration. Details of what was required to be recorded when registering a birth in a specific country can be discovered from *Abstract of Arrangements Respecting Registration of Births, Marriages and Deaths in the United Kingdom and the Other Countries of the British Commonwealth of Nations, and in the Irish Republic.* More recent addresses, fees for searches and copies and even replica application forms can be found in the *International Vital Records Handbook* by Thomas Jay Kemp.

Adoption

In the Miscellaneous Section of the ground floor of the Family Records Centre, there are the separate indexes to formal adoption in England and Wales. These date from 1927. As only the new name of the child, registered following the court order, is recorded, and this is usually dramatically different from the original name of the adoptee, they are not useful in researching the genealogy of the child's natural parents. Some children were adopted by their step-parents. If so, the names will have not been altered.

The adoption papers must be obtained to identify the name of the mother and, if married, her husband. They can only be accessed by the adopted person through the General Register Office, perhaps after due counselling. These papers will provide a date and place, allowing the original birth certificate to be sought.

Identifying the right birth

If candidates have been identified in the birth indexes for England and Wales, or in the Miscellaneous Section, certified copies of the birth registration can be ordered. This can be done online too, through *www.gro.gov.uk*, at a local register office for births in that district only by using *www.ukbmd.org.uk*, or by visiting the Family Records Centre. Some offices will produce copies following applications by post or telephone.

If more than one good candidate is found, use 'checking points' to narrow the search for the correct document.

The back of the birth application form used at the Family Records Centre allows additional information to be checked against the content of the registered copy. Checking points can also be used for online ordering. The most useful of these are date of birth, if known, or the father's forename(s). The latter is normally known if a marriage certificate has been found for the person whose birth is being sought, since this records the name and occupation of the fathers of both the groom and the bride. Beware that the father's forenames might not necessarily be recorded in the same order as was given by his son or daughter at their marriage. If you wish to check to see if the child was the son of Thomas, request that the father's name is shown as 'Thomas alone or with other names'. This will allow for that name to appear anywhere among those which the father used when registering the birth.

The place of birth or father's occupation is a much less reliable checking point. Children can be born in hospitals, maternity homes and work-houses, or even 'in the road'! Similarly, it cannot be expected that the person checking the original entry would be able to interpret and link an unusual version of an occupation against the more common description that you have sup-plied. Will they know that a clicker or a last maker or even a cordwainer was really a shoemaker? Both places of residence and father's occupation can change frequently over a short period of time.

You may be able to eliminate some of the possible births before paying for them to be checked. Some children may be shown to have died young because they appear in the death indexes, and obviously they cannot have grown up to become your ancestor. The baptisms of some of the children can be found in the indexes to post-1837 events (*see* International Genealogical Index on page 48 and British Isles Vital Records Index on page 46). If so, they may have a different father's name and can be eliminated as a candidate. If several of the births were registered in the same district, try that local office to see if the right entry can be identified.

If many candidates need to be checked, make use of a reference checking or verification sheet. These are available from the Information or Enquiry Desk. In conjunction with an ordinary application form for the first chosen reference, each sheet allows up to a further ten possibilities to be checked against the chosen fact. Most importantly, the initial outlay fee is much reduced. For 11 references, rather than paying, say, £77 if each application was separate, the fee would be only £37 (£7 for the first entry and 10 x £3 for the others). Enter the chosen references in descending order of likelihood and *always* tick the box that says 'stop at the first reference which agrees'. As soon as one entry is found which fits the chosen criteria, the copy will be produced and you will receive a refund of all the remaining fees that have been paid. You can then decide if the right entry has been found or if others need to be checked.

If your ancestor had a common name, it may be very difficult, if not expensive, to locate him or her. If he had a brother or sister with a much more distinctive name, who has been found in a census or a Family Bible, try for that child first. To find the reference to that registration may be much more straightforward. Obtain a copy and it will show the same parents as your direct ancestor! Remember, though, that the other child, the one you have found, may have been a half-brother or half-sister and not a full sibling. This strategy can be particularly useful if the birth of your ancestor was not registered or took place before 1837.

If you have found out from another source, such as a census, a family or printed source or a service record, where the registration probably took place, application can be made at the local register office. This may allow the entry to be obtained locally, if it was registered there.

If you think that a factual error has been introduced during the transcription and copying process, whilst the information was transferred from the local office to the Registrar General, it is worth going back to the beginning of the registration process. Obtain a copy of the same document from the local register office. There may be differences between the two versions of the same certified entry.

There is usually an index to the records of that local office. You can make searches at the local superintendent registrar's office for a statutory fee.

Baptismal records

If a child was born before the national registration system started in 1837, the baptism of the child would be recorded in a parish register if the family attended the Church of England. If the parents were of another religious denomination, their offspring will be found in the sources kept by that sect or faith. This may be a record of baptism or birth or of another religious rite, depending on what the denomination believed should be written down for posterity. Some non-conformists appear in Church of England records as well.

It must be remembered that church records did not come to an end when the state introduced civil registration. Religious sects continued to record those who had undergone their ceremonies long after 1837, even up to the present. The Church of England, together with other denominations, recorded the baptisms of its children. Other faiths recorded events which were more important to them, such as births, confirmations or circumcisions.

Thus if, for any of the reasons discussed already and despite all your efforts, a birth is not to be found in the indexes and records of civil registration and through the local registration districts and offices, a religious record of the child and his or her parents can still be sought.

Church of England

The baptismal records of the established Church of England, which also maintained the parochial structure throughout Wales, came into existence when Henry VIII took this country away from the Catholic Church in Rome in 1538. From that date, the parish registers should include the date of the baptism, the name(s) given to the child and the names and surname of the parents. Often only the father's Christian name is given. What was recorded was at the mercy of the incumbent or parish clerk. Bonus information may be the date of birth of the child or the maiden surname of the mother. After 1812, with Rose's Act, the format of the entries was stipulated, and to a certain extent limited, by the introduction of printed paper registers. The occupation of the father and a place of residence was now included.

Parish registers have mostly been deposited in county record offices. Abridged dates of the earliest and latest registers, which have been handed in to safe custody, are found in *The Phillimore Atlas & Index of Parish Registers* edited by Cecil Humphery-Smith. This includes only the pre-1832 parishes of England and Wales whose surviving registers to 1812 were surveyed and recorded in *The Parish Register Abstract* of 1831. These are deemed to be the 12,500 or so ancient parishes. Their geographical locality is illustrated on the individual county maps. The index section shows what finding aids exist to help you access the records of the parishioners. Also included for each county is a topographical map of 1834, which is particularly useful in envisaging the main routes of communication and the location of the main market towns that our ancestors may have frequented. This publication also includes Scotland.

In the next half-century after 1832, the rapidly growing population increased the need for new churches. In the Victorian era, many new parishes, each with its own church, were created out of the ancient parishes. The records of these Victorian parishes may also be found in the county record office.

The *National Index of Parish Registers* series, published by the Society of Genealogists, provides details about all Church of England parishes, both ancient and modern. This includes the date of foundation and the name of the parish from which it was separated. Information is also included about nonconformist places of worship.

Dade registers

Many parishes, mainly in the north-eastern counties of England, adopted a much more detailed and informative form of register. They were designed by William Dade, and were used from between 1770 and 1812. They record not only the date of baptism and parentage but a great deal of extra genealogical material. The position of the child in the family, such as '3rd son and 5th child', is noted, together with date of birth. The names of all four grandparents and their occupations and places of residence or birth are also recorded, as is information about two of the child's great-grandfathers, being the fathers of the two grandmothers.

If you are conducting searches at the end of the 18th and in the early 19th centuries in an area where Dade registers were used, you should extend your search of the baptismal records. You

Smart data: The Dade registers

The Dade registers were named after the Reverend William Dade, a clergyman in York, whose system recorded information in much greater detail than other registers. The far-seeing cleric wrote: 'This scheme ... will afford much clearer intelligence to the researches of posterity than the imperfect method hitherto.' In 1777, Archbishop William Markham introduced the Dade registration system throughout the Diocese of York, and it was adopted by about 200 parishes over the following 40 years. Reverend Barrington instigated the use of a slightly simpler version in Wiltshire, Bristol and Berkshire in 1783, while the Bishop of Durham followed suit in Durham in 1798. Unfortunately, in 1812 Rose's Act sounded the death knell for this wonderful innovation and goldmine for the genealogist.

may find siblings of your direct ancestor recorded in the detailed format. If they were, what a bonus! You will have learned how many older children there were in that family and their sexes. Most importantly, you will have been provided with a statement of who you are looking for in previous generations and even which parish registers are worth searching for them.

Access to registers

Once the office or library where the registers have been deposited has been ascertained, a visit can be made to make the required searches. Consult the website of the office. This can be done through *www.nationalarchives.gov.uk/archon* or *www.genuki.org.uk*. Learn about opening hours and any special access requirements which will make your visit more profitable. *Record Offices: How to Find Them* edited by Jeremy Gibson and Pamela Peskett can be valuable in finding your way to the relevant repository.

Do not forget to make an appointment and check whether a special reader's card or ticket is needed for access before setting off. If travelling from afar, choose a day when the office is open for the longest period. Book any necessary equipment, such as a microfilm or microfiche reader, or a table, depending on how the records are made available.

Some parishes churches have, of course, lost their records through theft, fire, war or the slow ravages of time. If so, and this is the parish where your ancestors chose to worship, to marry and to baptize their children, and where they were ultimately buried, the significant events in your genealogy may have been lost for ever.

Some churches have chosen to retain their records and have not deposited them in the county record office. If so, access to the records may be more difficult. The address of the incumbent can be obtained from the most recent *Crockford's Clerical Directory* or the county record office can advise. The results of the search may be obtained by letter or e-mail, or through a personal visit to the church, arranged in advance by appointment. A fee will probably be charged for access or a postal search.

If for any reason the parish registers are not available, have been lost or are deficient for the period under investigation, an alternative source of information is the annual copies of the entries in the parish registers. These were sent to the ecclesiastical authorities and are generally called bishops' transcripts. In some dioceses, there are two sets of such records. The other copy was returned to the archdeacon and these are called archdeacons' transcripts. Both sets of records are now to be found in the diocesan record office. This may or may not be the same as the county record office. A guide to the bishops' transcripts and archdeacons' transcripts for each diocese can be found in *Bishops' Transcripts and Marriage Licences, Bonds and Allegations* compiled by Jeremy Gibson.

It cannot be expected that all the transcripts will survive for a given parish. Just like any annual returns that must be filed, many did not find their way safely into the appropriate place in the records. Indeed, a diocese may have had a disaster where many, if not all, of its returns were lost through fire or decay in the place where they were stored. Where they have survived reasonably well, they provide another chance of finding a baptismal entry for that elusive ancestor. Usually the transcripts become much more patchy as the 19th century draws to a close.

Where two sets of transcripts exist, it can be the case that one set is stored in chronological order parish by parish. This is useful where all entries for a surname need to be extracted from a certain time period. The other set may be stored year by year, with all the returns for each parish within a deanery being kept together. Such a collection can be of greatest interest when the approximate year of a particular event is known, such as a person's birth, but the parish is yet to be determined. A wide geographical area can be quickly searched within a few years of records.

Copies of records

Since the records were created, a copy of the parish registers or bishops' transcripts may have been made. This more recent copy dates from anywhere from the 19th century to the present. It may be handwritten, typed or printed, and may cover a large time period or only a few years. It may include all three types of event – baptisms, marriages and burials – or just one sort of record. Most importantly, it may have been indexed by surname. Many copies of the transcript may exist. If so, one of these may be more accessible or closer to your home than the original. An indexed transcription may allow a more efficient search to be made.

Copies of the transcripts will be located in local or national libraries or the record office itself, or may have been collected by a genealogical organization. The Society of Genealogists holds the largest collection, having a transcript for some part of the records of about 10,000 of the 12,500 or so ancient parishes. The *National Index of Parish Registers* series, published by the Society of Genealogists, states where any transcriptions or copies can be searched.

If a secondary copy is used and the entries being sought are found using the internal index, you will have saved yourself a great deal of searching through the original. If the entry is not found, you should still search the text of the transcript. Do not rely on the transcriber or indexer being perfect.

Many errors were made in reading the original entry and just as many in producing the index to the transcription. If in doubt, go back to the original parish register. The entry may just have been left out by mistake! Anything that you find in a transcription should be checked against the original.

Protestant nonconformists

Many other denominations kept records from the time they were formed. These may have been records of birth or baptism and, in some cases, death or burial. If it is believed, for any reason, that the family may not have attended or used the Church of England, records of other possible religious sects must be tried. The most likely clue is that a post-1837 marriage certificate shows that the ceremony took place in a nonconformist chapel or other religious building. Of course, the births of children of nonconformists should be registered in the usual way after 1 July 1837 and be found in the national indexes that are at the Family Records Centre.

Many nonconformist Protestant records were deposited with the Registrar General in 1837 and some others in 1858. These are now at the National Archives and at the Family Records Centre in classes of RG 4 to RG 6 and RG 8. They are available on microfilm. These include Congregationalists, Baptists, Presbyterians, Methodists, Huguenots, Quakers and Independents and other smaller sects. There are a few Catholic registers. Most have been filmed and abstracted by the Church of Jesus Christ of Latter-day Saints (Mormon Church) and most appear on the International Genealogical Index (*see* page 48). The International Genealogical Index does not index Quaker registers.

Records post-1837 may still remain with the relevant church or chapel or may have been deposited in the county record office. Copies of the registers may be found in record offices, libraries, the Society of Genealogists or the archives or libraries of the particular denomination.

To learn more about the records of a given denomination, use the *My Ancestor* series of publications produced by the Society of Genealogists (*see* the reading list at the end of the chapter).

From the mid-18th century, Protestant non-conformists attempted to set up systems for the registration of the births of their children. The most widely used was that which was established at Dr Williams' Library in Red Cross Street, London, in 1742. From then until 1837, parents who lived not only in the capital city but all over England and Wales, recorded nearly 50,000 births. It provides a centralized source for the births of some of the children of parents who were not adherents to the Church of England. Their local record of birth or baptism may have been lost or not recorded. If the parents chose to take advantage of this new method of registration, which predated the state system by 95 years, this can be an invaluable, if not unique, way for us to find a record of the parentage of a nonconformist child. Many entries were made long after the birth of the child, so do not search just around the suspected year of birth.

The indexes are at the National Archives and Family Records Centre in class RG 4 on microfilm. Once the entry has been found, it will allow access to a very detailed form of birth certificate in RG 5. This will record the names of both parents, including the mother's maiden surname. It usually includes the address where the family lived, occupations and the name of the maternal grandfather. A second system of nonconformist registration was the Metropolitan Wesleyan Registry. It began in 1818, but many entries were made retrospectively back to 1777. Its records are also in RG 4 and RG 5.

Since the records of both of these two non-conformist systems are included in the British Isles Vital Records Index (2nd edition) on CD-ROM, produced by the Church of Jesus Christ of Latter-day Saints, do not forget to use this very useful supplement to the International Genea-logical Index. They are not in the International Genealogical Index itself. Indeed, the British Isles Vital Records Index entry may lead the researcher straight to the appropriate certificate in RG 5, this number being included.

Catholics, Quakers and Jews

Catholic baptismal records may be far more difficult to locate, especially in the 16th and 17th centuries, due to the continued persecution and lack of tolerance of its members. Church regi-sters, mainly of baptism, usually remain in the custody of the parish priest. Copies have been made and many have been published by the Catholic Record Society. Copies can be viewed at the Catholic Central Library or in the library of the Society of Genealogists. Few of the records have been deposited and consequently indexed in the International Genealogical Index.

An excellent guide to where registers and the copies can be found is Michael Gandy's *Catholic Missions and Registers 1700–1880*. If you need to contact the parish priest, his address can be obtained from the latest Catholic Year Book. Contact the Catholic Family History Society at *www.catholic-history.org.uk*.

Records of the births of Quakers are best accessed through the Quaker Digests. These consolidated the records of the local Monthly Meeting. The Digests, which cover separate geographical areas, each including a number of counties, can be viewed at Friends' House, in the local county record office or at the Society of Genealogists. Some have been published. Friends' House holds a national index to 1959. If an entry is found, the original entry can be viewed at the National Archives or the Family Records Centre in class RG 6. Once again, they are not included in the International Genealogical Index. The Society of Genealogists has produced *My Ancestors Were Quakers* by E.H. Milligan and M.J. Thomas. The Quaker Family History Society can be contacted at *www.qfhs.co.uk*.

If your ancestor was Jewish, there will, of course, be no baptismal records. The circumciser or mohel kept the circumcision records. These can be almost impossible to locate. Other sources for Jewish genealogy are much more important. These include probate records and monumental inscriptions (*see* Chapter 7). *My Ancestors Were Jewish: How Can I Find Out More about Them?* by A. Joseph should be consulted. The Jewish Genealogical Society of Great Britain, *www.jgsgb.org.uk*, will be of great assistance.

Finding aids and indexes

You have found a reference to your ancestor from census returns dating from 1851 (the 1841 enumeration does not record a parish of birth), but no baptism can be found there. Place of birth and place of baptism are not necessarily the same. What next? There are a number of readily accessible indexes to baptisms.

The main port of call for most genealogists and family historians is the International Genealogical Index. Compiled by the Church of Jesus Christ of Latter-day Saints (the Mormons), it can be very valuable in locating baptisms and even some births (together with possible marriages for the parents, even if the baptism is not included). It includes the baptismal records of many parishes of the Church of England, taken from either the registers or the bishops' transcripts or both, depending on what the Church has micro-filmed. The Index also includes the great majority of the Protestant nonconformist records in class RG 4 at the National Archives or the Family Records Centre, which were deposited in 1837. Other sources, such as the records of some workhouses and the main London lying-in hos-pitals, are also to be found there. The Index records only names of the parents and child, the parish or place of baptism (or birth) and its date. The original entry may contain much more information. It should always be viewed in the original form.

The International Genealogical Index can be searched online through the FamilySearch web-site *www.familysearch.org*. The CD version can also be used in major libraries and record offices. Searches can be filtered by location, time period or other criteria to reduce the number of reported results. Wildcard searches can be made. Once a baptism has been found, use the 'parent search' facility to find the couple's other children or, at least, children whose parents had the same com-bination of names. Be careful, as entries where a mother's maiden name was recorded will be separate from those where such additional information was not included. Lists of candidates can be printed out.

The computerized versions rely on the machine answering a specific question, so it is sometimes useful to return to the last version that was produced on microfiche (1992), where you may spot an entry that the computer has not provided. This microfiche version is usually available in libraries and record offices too. You can print out all entries for a name in a particular county section. Often, you will spot a relevant baptism which the computer had not reported to you.

If a possible candidate is found, the source of the entry is of great significance. You need to know if the entry was placed in the index as a result of the microfilming and abstraction process of the Church of Jesus Christ of Latter-day Saints. These tend to be more accurate and reliable. Alternatively, a Mormon who has traced a pedigree may have submitted the entry. These entries are sometimes less accurate, if not misleading. The source of the information is shown in the electronic forms of the index.

On the microfiche version, the abstraction entries have a source number prefixed with a letter. Those submitted by a Mormon will have an 'all-figure' number.

Check all entries back to the original parish register or bishops' transcript to which the entry is attributed. If it is a personal entry, the name of the submitter can be located and the research records ordered through the Church of Jesus Christ of Latter-day Saints at its family history centres.

Do not always believe the annotation of 'child' which sometimes is included. Although this purports to indicate that there is some evidence that the child died early in life, no detailed research has been conducted to confirm this connection between the baptism and a later burial in the same source. Of course, such warnings should be borne in mind and all precautions taken before accepting such an entry as ancestral.

If using the disk or online version of the International Genealogical Index, also try the Ancestral File and Pedigree Resource File sections of FamilySearch. These include clues and information that were found by the Mormons whilst conducting their own research. They may be dates of birth or baptism not found in parochial or state records, perhaps found in private papers or the Family Bible.

As the International Genealogical Index does not include the records of either of the two nonconformist registries, you must also use its supplement, the British Isles Vital Records Index (2nd edition). This is only available on compact disk and not by using online access.

There are also a number of baptismal indexes which cover a whole county or a few parishes in an area for a given time period. These can often make the research process much more efficient. If an index exists, it should be listed in *Specialist Indexes for Family Historians* by Jeremy Gibson and Elizabeth Hampson. Many of these have been collected together by the Federation of Family History Societies and can be accessed, very inexpensively, through *www.familyhistoryonline.net*. For London, from 1780 to 1837, try the surviving part of Pallot's Baptism Index. This is available on CD or online through *www.ancestry.co.uk*.

Ripple method

If no baptism for your ancestor is found in a baptismal index, the search must be extended to other parishes where the ceremony may have taken place.

Usually, our ancestors married before the births and subsequent baptisms of their children. By using the much more frequently produced indexes to marriages or to marriage licences, bonds and allegations, it may be possible to home in on other areas where the union of the parents might have taken place, or where the surname is more commonly found. Such searches and indexes are discussed in Chapter 3. Localizing the surname can be done where there is an index to a reasonably large geographical area in a relevant time period. Even if the surname is fairly common, marriage entries can be selected based on any unusual forenames that may be found frequently among the later generations. These are likely to have occurred in, and been passed down from, an earlier generation.

If this type of search does not lead you to the place of origin of the previous generation, you may have no choice but to extend the search systematically from the last parish where the family is known to have lived or worshipped. This is the ripple method of searching. It is equivalent to throwing a stone into a pond. As the ripples spread, the number of parishes equidistant from the later home of the family increases considerably. Before searching all the parishes in your circle, you should check which are supposed to be included in a given index or finding aid, and first try those parishes that are not included. The index section of *The Phillimore Atlas & Index of*

Parish Registers can help with this. Remember that the coverage is not always complete. Do not assume that both baptisms and marriages for any one parish are included, especially in the International Genealogical Index.

If in doubt, you should search all those parishes that border on the parish where the family was last found or where the marriage of the bride or groom took place. It is quite likely that they originated within a ten-mile radius. Take into account the main routes of communication and the physical barriers to easy travel. Bear in mind what other factors encouraged our ancestors to migrate for an economic or social reason.

There may be other records produced during the lives of ancestors that provide clues to where they had been born. These will be examined in subsequent chapters, considering each aspect and time period of their later career.

Bastardy

If your ancestor was illegitimate in the 17th to 19th centuries, the person filling in the register might have recorded the name of the putative or reputed father. Of course, there was no genetic testing available then to confirm whether or not that man was the proven father. Rather, this was the man whom society, or the woman herself, believed to be the most likely sire.

If such a statement is found or if the child was assigned no father, try to find other sources that record whom he might have been. The parish register may simply state that Mary Jones had an illegitimate, base-born or spurious child, who was baptized. Was she later required to reveal its paternity?

Before 1834, the Overseers of the Poor and churchwardens of the parish might have questioned the woman to try to elicit whom she believed had made her pregnant. This bastardy examination may survive and result in the production of a bastardy bond. This formally decreed which man would be financially responsible for the expenses of the birth and the child's upkeep. He would pay so much per week until other ways could be found of ensuring that the child did not become a drain on parish funds (*see* Poor Law Apprenticeship in Chapter 2). This was the 18th- and 19th-century version of the Child Support Agency.

If the putative father ran away to escape his duty and avoid paying for what may have been another man's child, a bastardy warrant would be issued to apprehend him and enforce his newly found responsibility. These documents would have been stored with the other parish paperwork in the parish chest, a secure wooden trunk in the church. If they have survived, the bastardy papers will have been deposited in the county record office along with other parish material, including the church registers themselves. They will be catalogued separately but should not be neglected if paternity is sought. Of course, such documentation generally only exists for the lower classes, which had no independent means of support. Unfortunately, the records might not have survived the ravages of time and the tidiness of the vicar's wife.

Reference to the processes behind the search for the name of the father of an illegitimate child will also be in the records of the Quarter Sessions. This tier of the legal system was mainly responsible for imposition of the Poor Laws (*see* Chapter 5). If the original documents have not survived, it is possible to find mention of an enquiry into the birth of an illegitimate child. Although it will be less informative, you will learn that Mary Jones had a base-born child and that a bastardy order was issued against John Fowler. His name might not have been recorded at the child's baptism.

Since the couple had also broken church law by committing fornication, the ecclesiastical court might also have taken a great interest in the birth. It may be that a 'process' was pursued against the unhappy couple, taking evidence from witnesses or deponents who had seen the couple behaving in far too friendly a manner. This may again provide good circumstantial evidence of the father of the child. Such records are to be found in the diocesan record office (*see* Chapter 5).

Smart reading on birth records

Abstract of Arrangements Respecting Registration of Births, Marriages and Deaths in the United Kingdom and the Other Countries of the British Commonwealth of Nations, and in the Irish Republic (General Register Office / HMSO, 1952)

Bishops' Transcripts and Marriage Licences, Bonds and Allegations, by Jeremy Gibson, 5th edn (Federation of Family History Societies, 2001)

The British Overseas: A Guide to Records of Their Baptisms, Births, Marriages, Deaths and Burials Available in the United Kingdom, by Geoffrey Yeo, revised by Philippa Smith, 3rd edn (Guildhall Library, 1994)

Catholic Missions and Registers 1700–1880, by Michael Gandy (Society of Genealogists, 1993), 6 vols and atlas

International Vital Records Handbook, by Thomas Jay Kemp, 4th edn (Genealogical Publishing, 2000)

My Ancestors Were Baptists, by G.R. Breed, 4th edn (Society of Genealogists, 2002)

My Ancestors Were Congregationalists in England and Wales, by D.J.H. Clifford, 2nd edn (Society of Genealogists, 1997)

My Ancestors Were English Presbyterians/ Unitarians, by A. Ruston, 2nd edn (Society of Genealogists, 2001)

My Ancestors Were in the Salvation Army, by R. Wiggins, 2nd edn (Society of Genealogists, 1999)

My Ancestors Were Inghamites, by P.J. Oates (Society of Genealogists, 2003)

My Ancestors Were Jewish: How Can I Find Out More about Them?, by A. Joseph, 4th edn (Society of Genealogists, 2005)

My Ancestors Were Methodists, by W. Leary, 4th edn (Society of Genealogists, 2005)

My Ancestors Were Quakers, by E.H. Milligan and M.J. Thomas, 3rd edn (Society of Genealogists, 2005)

The Phillimore Atlas & Index of Parish Registers, by Cecil Humphery-Smith (ed.), 3rd edn (Phillimore, 2003)

Record Offices: How to Find Them, edited by Jeremy Gibson and Pamela Peskett, 9th edn (Federation of Family History Societies, 2002)

Specialist Indexes for Family Historians, by Jeremy Gibson and Elizabeth Hampson, 2nd edn (Federation of Family History Societies, 2000)

Tracing Your Ancestors in the Public Record Office, by Amanda Bevan, 6th edn (Public Register Office, 2002); 7th edn, forthcoming (the National Archives, 2006)

Chapter 2

Out of school

- Schooling
- Colleges and universities
- Vocational training and apprenticeships
- Merchant companies and guilds
- Poor Law apprenticeships

One rewarding way of discovering more about ancestors is by searching for information on how they learnt the skills that they used later on in life. This can provide new clues to parentage or place of birth. Your research may also reveal fascinating insights into how he or she lived during the first 20 years of life before settling down to earn a wage and start a family.

Schooling

Most of our ancestors, especially before the Education Act of 1870, received no formal schooling. Training and learning were based in the home, possibly at church or Sunday school, and by acquiring the skills needed to take up a trade or profession. This was often through apprenticeship.

Formal school education was the prerogative of the upper classes. Many ancient private and public schools were established through charitable bequests and royal patronage. Guilds and livery companies founded schools too. Many of these have produced or published their alumni registers or lists of those who went there. Such records provide some genealogical information about the students admitted and often detail their later careers. Poorer children may have been admitted through scholarship or charitable bequests each year, even into some of the top institutions.

For the masses, some education became available from about 1810 through the Church of England, nonconformist sects and at Ragged and Dame Schools. When provision for regular learning was strengthened by the 1870 Education Act, most children attended regularly. Schools in each parish are listed in commercial directories and *The Victoria Histories of the Counties of England* with their date of foundation (*see* Chapter 3). For a history of schooling and its records see *The Growth of British Education and its Records* by Colin Chapman.

Surviving admission and attendance registers and log books will record the more noteworthy events in the day-to-day life of schools, their teachers and students. Punishment books can tell us what our ancestors got up to behind the bike sheds. Admission and discharge registers provide ages or dates of birth, addresses and names of parents. By using these records, you may be able to identify family groups. Children of the same parents probably attended the same school. You can learn when and why your ancestors left. They might have gone to another school or been forced to start work to support the family. Many school records remain with the institution, if it is still in existence. Many others have been deposited in county record offices.

The larger companies, guilds and charities set up schools and would have maintained records of the foundations that they endowed. *City Livery Companies and Related Organisations* catalogues school records for educational institutions set up by the companies of the City of London.

Colleges and universities

Until the mid-19th century, university and college education was open to very few. Oxford and Cambridge were the only universities in existence in England until 1832. They attracted people studying to be clerics, lawyers and doctors, as well as the sons of the aristocracy. The Alumni Cantabrigienses for Cambridge are published from 'the earliest times to 1900' and the Alumni Oxonienses for the University of Oxford are published from 1500 to 1886. The website of *www.ancestry.co.uk* includes the records for those who attended Cambridge University.

Later, training colleges and the 19th-century universities catered for the new, more educated classes. They produced ministers of the church, both Anglican and nonconformist, as well as

---

Smart data: Alumni

Students who have attended a particular school, college or university are called alumni. Lists of alumni have been published for many educational establishments, both independent and state. They often include detailed biographical and genealogical information about the scholar. His or her dates of attendance and educational attainment are recorded, and sometimes his or her parentage, and date and place of birth. The later life of the alumnus may also be described. This can include a spouse, children, notable career achievements and ultimate fate. Reference is often made to a more detailed account of their life or an obituary, and this can lead the family historian to other sources.

---

teachers. If you are able to examine the alumni registers or lists of those who trained at such bodies, they may provide interesting genealogical information. Write to the educational institution itself to discover additional data.

To learn what is available in print, consult P.M. Jacobs, *Registers of the Universities, Colleges and Schools of Great Britain and Northern Ireland*. Use the large collection of printed and manuscript material housed at the Society of Genealogists. *School, University and College Registers and Histories in the Library of the Society of Genealogists* lists what is held there.

Vocational training and apprenticeships

Those who did not receive formal schooling, as we would recognize it today, learnt their trade on the job. A local tradesman or employer would take on an apprentice to pass on his skills. Some signed up to voluntary agreements between the master, the parents and the apprentice. Such indentures set down the terms of the relationship between master and trainee, including what the apprentice could and couldn't do and what the master was supposed to provide in terms of tuition and upkeep. As they were not centrally registered, these agreements, being family papers, have often been lost. Some for London were saved in the collections made by Crisp and Clench. Some 1,500 indentures, dating from the 17th to the 19th centuries, are preserved at the Society of Genealogists. Other original agreements exist by chance in county record offices and family and business archives.

From 1710 to 1811, apprenticeship bindings were taxed. The records, known as Apprenticeship Books, are found at the National Archives in class IR 1. They are far from complete for all agreements signed in this period. The collection is really a lucky dip. Not all types of apprenticeship were subject to taxation; only those where the tax was greater than one shilling were included. This sum was calculated as a percentage of the binding fee. Often those where the master was a parent or another relative were exempt. Where the arrangement was through the Overseers of the Poor (*see* below), these will not be included in the registers or ledgers.

The taxation records are indexed from 1710 to 1774 by the Society of Genealogists in *The Apprentices of Great Britain.* You can search it at the Society of Genealogists or at the National Archives in IR 17. It is also available on microfiche or online through *www.britishorigins.com*. The index includes the date of the indenture, the name of the apprentice, the name of the father (or, if he is dead, that of the widowed mother) and where they lived, the name and trade of the master and the binding fee. Little more information is available by returning to the original records through the reference to the piece number and folio. For 1775 to 1811, there is no index to apprentices or masters, and a search must be made in IR 1 to see if there is a reference to the apprenticeship of an ancestor.

As it is often known where someone settled

down after training, the index can provide a unique link to where the boy or girl and the parents lived at the time of entering into vocational training.

Merchant companies and guilds

Other apprentices were trained through one of the merchant, guild or livery companies, whether it was in London or in any one of the main cities and boroughs. Some places became famous for, and centres of, particular crafts or products – for example, Worcester for gloves and porcelain, Sheffield for steel and cutlery and Northampton for shoes. Other cities or towns had a general guild for all the merchants and their apprentices who traded within the environs of that urban area. Each became a magnet for teenagers to learn a skill that would elevate them out of a potential labouring existence.

Apprenticeship often began at 14 and lasted for about 7 years or until the age of 21. In some cases, apprenticeship began much earlier. Boys as young as 7 could join the Royal Navy. After satisfying their master, those training on land could become a freeman of the guild, company or city. They were then free to vote, take on their own apprentices and continue the passage of knowledge. This was a great step up in life (*see* Chapter 6).

Records of apprenticeship can be found in county record offices. Those for companies of London are mainly in Guildhall Library. Some companies have retained their own records, although there may be copies or films of the registers at Guildhall Library.

City Livery Companies and Related Organisations includes details of all the deposited records for each company. Category C records are those of the members of the company. Here will be found lists of apprenticeship bindings and freedom admissions together with details of any surname indexes with their reference numbers. A more detailed list is available at the enquiry desk in the library. Some records are on microfilm whilst others are only available in document form. The holdings can be researched online at *www.history.ac.uk/gh/livlist.htm*.

There may be unique types of records. One company, the Watermen and Lightermen, whose members were particularly mobile as they had waterborne transport, has an unusual additional source called Apprentice Affidavits. They date from 1759 and record the date and place of the birth or baptism of the apprentice. If the information is correct, this can lead you immediately to the baptism, and hence the parentage, of someone who trained to practise this trade.

If your ancestors are from other parts of the country, search the original and published lists of those who signed up to apprenticeship in other centres of commerce. If a man is known to have settled in a town or city, these records are a very valuable source of genealogical information.

The apprenticeship records of many cities and towns have been indexed by surname. The finding aids can be found in *Occupational Sources for Genealogists* by Stuart Raymond or through his individual county guides, if published, in the *British Genealogical Bibliographies* series by the Federation of Family History Societies.

Someone may have compiled an index to local apprenticeship records or those of a particular trade or occupation, but it may not have been published and may remain with the compiler. The occupations section of *Specialist Indexes for Family Historians* by Jeremy Gibson and Elizabeth Hampson will lead you to such valuable sources.

Cliff Webb has indexed the records of many London companies in his *London Apprentices* volumes at the Society of Genealogists. These have now been integrated into the British Origins Database at *www.britishorigins.com*. Printed sources for London apprentices are included in

Stuart Raymond's *Londoners' Occupations: A Genealogical Guide*.

In addition to having become free of a company or guild, the person you seek may have become a freeman of the City of London. You need to look for your ancestor in the 14 index volumes to these freemen, previously held by the Corporation of London Record Office and now at the London Metropolitan Archives. These 14 volumes are a semi-alphabetical index (by initial letter of the surname only, and then in chrono-logical order) in 14 separate time periods from 1681 to 1940, showing the name of the freeman, his date of freedom of the City of London and the company to which he belonged.

The associated papers for those admitted, following apprenticeship or servitude, give information about the father of the child and the master who was responsible for his training. You will learn the name of the company to which the freeman belonged and so will be able to search the records of that organization at Guildhall Library. Using this method, the place of residence of the parents of the apprentice may be discovered.

Poor Law apprenticeships

For those further down the social scale, apprenticeship and training may have come in a much less voluntary and pleasant manner. Before 1834, the Overseers of the Poor were responsible for dealing with orphan or poor children living in their parish. If necessary, they could farm the children out to a local tradesman or farmer to prevent them from becoming a drain on the poor relief coffers. The master would then be responsible for their training and their day-to-day food, apparel and lodging. Often this proved to be hardly more than slavery with little or no actual training. Some charities also placed poor children in apprenticeships.

The bindings are recorded in ledgers, found among the Poor Law records of the parish. They are usually deposited in the appropriate county record office and should record parentage. The individual indentures may also survive. Children as young as 7 could be sentenced to serve their master until they reached the age of 24, or were allowed to marry.

The records of the Quarter Sessions may include references to those involved in the Poor Law system of apprenticeship. Such material can be accessed at the county record office through

Quarter Session Records for Family Historians: A Select List by Jeremy Gibson. You may be able to find the names included in such documents through *www.a2a.org.uk.*

The records of training, apprenticeship and education can often provide you with vital information about the place of birth and parentage of the child. This may lead you to that elusive birth or baptism. If not, you should consider later aspects of the person's life and career.

Smart reading on education records

British Genealogical Bibliographies, by Stuart Raymond (Federation of Family History Societies)

City Livery Companies and Related Organisations, 3rd edn (Guildhall Library, 1989)

The Growth of British Education and its Records, by Colin Chapman, 2nd edn (Lochin, 1992)

Londoners' Occupations: A Genealogical Guide, by Stuart Raymond, 2nd edn (Federation of Family History Societies, 2001)

Occupational Sources for Genealogists, by Stuart Raymond, 2nd edn (Federation of Family History Societies, 1996)

Quarter Session Records for Family Historians: A Select List, by Jeremy Gibson, 4th edn (Federation of Family History Societies, 1995)

Registers of the Universities, Colleges and Schools of Great Britain and Northern Ireland, by P.M. Jacobs (Athlone Press, 1964)

School, University and College Registers and Histories in the Library of the Society of Genealogists, 2nd edn (Society of Genealogists, 1996)

Specialist Indexes for Family Historians, by Jeremy Gibson and Elizabeth Hampson, 2nd edn (Federation of Family History Societies, 2000)

Chapter 3

Settling down

- Marriages after 1837
- Where and when?
- The importance of the marriage certificate
- Access to certificates
- Records outside England and Wales
- Marriages before 1837
- Marriage indexes
- Banns or licence?
- Divorce
- Census returns
- Census indexes
- Original returns

After your ancestor learned a skill or trade to allow him to earn a living or at least eke out an existence, the time came to find a mate, to settle down and to start the next generation. This may or may not have involved marriage. Usually, if the couple did not formally wed, the offspring of such a union would be recorded without the father's name: the child would be deemed illegitimate.

After the start of civil registration in 1837, sometimes both parents, although not legally married, would choose to go together to register the births of their children. If married, a woman could record only her husband as the legal father of her child, even if the offspring was the result of a liaison with another man. After 1874, for another man to be assigned the paternity of her child, he had to have accepted that responsibility by visiting the registrar with her and acting with her as joint informant. Both names would be recorded on the certificate, which is indexed under both surnames. In general, since we are more frequently descended from married ancestors, there should be a record of their union.

Marriages after 1837

From 1 July 1837, all marriages should have been solemnized at either a religious or a civil ceremony. Apart from the traditional method of marrying in a church or other denominational building, it became possible from that time for people to marry without any religious ceremony at the register office. The marriage was conducted by the registrar. This was particularly common and popular with nonconformists since, except for Quakers and Jews, they had been forced to marry according to the rites of the Church of England following Lord Hardwicke's Marriage Act of 1753. This included Roman Catholics. Now they could avoid this intrusion on their wedding. The registration districts had been principally based on the Poor Law Unions that had been formed in 1834. There was a rather unfortunate link between being one of the lower classes, subject to examination and removal back to your parish of settlement if you were unable to provide for yourself and your family, and the register office. There was a concern that the register office would impose the Poor Law, and thus people avoided going there to get married. This made civil ceremonies less popular in the early years.

Until 1898, although nonconformist buildings could be licensed for marriages, the registrar would need to be present to make the ceremony legal. After that, a nonconformist minister could become the person authorized to perform and register marriages.

There were two volumes of the church register and marriages were recorded by the clergy in both. One volume was sent quarterly to the superintendent registrar and then on to the Registrar General. The other volume was kept by the church and deposited with the superintendent registrar when it was full. It joined the records of any churches in that district which had been closed down. The original parish register will probably have been deposited at the county record office or remain with the church.

Thus, the copy which is produced for you from the national collection is a version of the original entry. It is written in the hand of the person who performed the ceremony or his clerk. However, the signatures of the two parties and the witnesses will not be in the original handwriting.

Errors can be introduced in any copying process. It would be foolish to believe that the copy, produced centrally from the records held at Southport, is necessarily identical to the original entry in the church register. The ages of the bride and groom could have mutated, or their marital status and even their names may have been incorrectly sent to the Registrar General.

If you believe that an error has been made, go back as far as possible along the transcription trail. Return to the original entry in the county record office or perhaps it is still held by the church or chapel, if the register has not been deposited. If it was a civil ceremony, obtain the registrar's copy.

Unlike births and deaths, there may not be a cumulative index to marriages which took place in that district. The records were sent in separately from each individual building where the ceremonies were performed. Thus, unless you know the particular church or chapel where the wedding took place, you may not be able to obtain a copy locally.

Remember that the ecclesiastical recording of marriages did not end in 1837. Rather, it was often the source of the state version. The centralized copy, which was sent to the Registrar General, can be obtained through the Family Records Centre or online through the office in Southport, but you do not have to use it. If you know where the marriage ceremony was performed, you may avoid paying the statutory fee for a certified copy. You can photocopy or print out the entry in the county record office where the register is deposited and is available on film or fiche.

Where and when?

Many of our ancestors married many miles from where we believe they lived. The groom may have been in one of the armed services or in a mobile trade or profession, or the couple may simply have eloped because the parents of the bride did not approve of him.

We often do not know when our ancestors married. Did the marriage take place 10, 20 or even 30 years before the date of birth of the child that we know of? Often it was less than nine months. Perhaps they waited until after all their children had been born before they made their union legal. This could have been because one person was still married to someone else and was not free to marry their present partner, and perhaps they had to await a divorce or the death of their spouse before another ceremony could take place. If so, we may need to look for 20 years after the birth date and registration of a child, who was recorded as though the parents were legally married. Many of our ancestors muddied the waters to avoid embarrassment. Do not always believe that a 'spinster' or 'bachelor' had not been married before.

How old were they when they married? We usually assume, when starting a marriage search in the records of civil registration, that they were between 19 and 30 years old. Some were much older and some considerably younger. If the ages of the couple are known from their deaths or from a census, do not fall into the trap of thinking that they could not marry before they were 18. In 1929, the legal age for marriage was raised to 16. Before then, the legal age for marriage with parental consent was only 14 for boys and 12 for girls. Although it is a rare occurrence to find a 13-year-old girl marrying in Britain, it seems to have been far more common among the British in India.

The importance of the marriage certificate

Why are we seeking a marriage certificate? Because this is one of the most informative documents in genealogical research. It is often possible to make do without a certified birth entry, learning the parentage from the record of baptism or a census return. However, the record of the post-1837 marriage provides the name, if known, of the father of both parties. An added bonus is his occupation and a statement of whether he was dead by the date of marriage of his son or daughter. If these clues are not discovered, how can we be reasonably sure that we have identified the appropriate birth or baptism? The name of the father and a continuity of a similar trade or profession adds to our confidence. If it was not necessary for John Smith to record the name and occupation of his father when he got married, we could not identify the correct record of his birth or baptism. We would probably not be able to proceed further with the search for his genealogy. If Mary Smith has a father called Shadrach, we are on much firmer ground. Even if the father was plain Joseph, but was shown at both the marriage and birth registration of his daughter to have been a wheelwright, we can be confident that we have found the right woman.

We are certainly interested in knowing whether the father of the bride or groom was described as 'dead' or 'deceased'. If so, we can begin a search for his death or burial before the date of the marriage of his child. However, if he was not stated to be dead, this does not mean that he was definitely alive at the time. It was not required that the word 'deceased' be recorded, although it was included in the 'Suggestions for the Guidance of the Clergy' and the 'Rules and Regulations' for 'Authorized Persons'. Do not jump to the conclusion that the father of a 70-year-old groom was alive when his son married because no statement of his previous demise was made.

The names of the witnesses to the union are also very valuable. They may be close relatives of the married couple. Finding a relationship through later research can prove that the correct family has been identified. A woman with a different surname may have been a married sister or aunt of the bride or groom.

Access to certificates

Unfortunately, the national indexes of marriage are sometimes less than helpful. From the September quarter of 1910 to the present day, second and additional names are only shown as initials. At least the surname of the other spouse is included from the beginning of 1912. This prevents the need for the systematic cross-referencing process required from 1837 to 1911. You can access the indexes through *www.1837 online.com* and *www.bmdindex. co.uk*.

The internet indexes available at *www.family relatives.org* allow you to search for a marriage over a long time period without having to examine each quarterly volume. By searching for both parties, a cross-reference between them will be found. You can obtain listings of all those with a given name who married in a certain time span. If the name is common, the search can be restricted to a geographical area.

Access to indexes to particular counties, areas or registration districts over particular time periods can be achieved through *www.ukbmd.org.uk*. It must be remembered that these indexes were produced locally. They may include entries not found in the national version of the indexes.

The use of *http://freebmd.rootsweb.com* can also avoid a systematic search through many quarterly volumes of the national indexes, seeking a cross-reference between two people, especially if each has a very common name. Once again, the search can be restricted to those who married in a geographical area or a registration district. It is also particularly useful when no apparent cross-reference between groom and bride is found in the General Register Office indexes. Use wildcard searches to find candidates that are listed with slightly different versions of the surname. If only one partner is noted, the researcher can click on the 'page number' link and view the names of the other people who have that same reference number. The other spouse may be identified, even if recorded with a variant of the surname or if the name has been misread or misindexed. For instance, Hull may have been misread as Stall. Finding such an error in interpretation would be almost impossible through conventional searching.

This index is also a good 'lucky dip' way of finding relatives whose marriages are not specifically being sought. Sometimes an unknown remarriage of an ancestor is spotted. If this union relates to a person who had previously married before 1837, the entry would prove invaluable. It will provide the name of the father, which would not have been recorded at the first marriage.

Once a possible candidate has been found, a certified copy can be obtained. If necessary, this can be ordered online through *www.gro.gov.uk*. Use checking points to select those who agree with known criteria. Particularly useful is a check for the second forename, which the indexes only show as an initial (September quarter of 1910 onwards). You can also make a selection based on the father's name, if known, or the marital status of the bride or groom, if seeking the remarriage of a widow(er) or someone who has been divorced.

If many candidates are found, the efficiency of the checking process can be enhanced and the initial outlay decreased by using checking or verification sheets (*see* Chapter 1). You may stipulate that the certified copy is to be produced only if the other spouse has a particular forename. Use this when no cross-reference is identified but several good candidates have been found for one party.

Records outside England and Wales

As with births, it must be remembered that the marriage being sought, if indeed it took place at all, may have happened outside England and Wales. The couple may have married elsewhere in the British Isles (*see* Chapters 1 and 7 for the dates of commencement of registration in each separate area). Many eloped to Scotland or the Channel Islands where marriage laws were less strict than in England.

Perhaps the marriage took place in another Commonwealth country. Thousands married on the Indian sub-continent or, indeed, anywhere in the world where the British traded or visited. It may be very difficult to find the marriage without some other family information about where the event took place. A census may reveal that the oldest child was born in a certain country. The trade, profession or occupation of the groom may provide some clues as to where to try next.

The record of the marriage may have been notified to the authorities in this country through the Consular Service or the Army. The main series are:

Consular marriages	1849–1965
Army marriages	1796–1965
Marriages abroad	1966 onwards

You can also search these through *www.1837 online.com*.

It should be noted that there are many other regimental marriages held by the Overseas Section that are not included in the printed volume of the indexes. Application should be made through the Family Records Centre if it is believed that the marriage took place when the groom was serving in the Army. You would need to know his regiment and an approximate year.

The India Office Records in the Asia, Pacific and Africa Collections in the British Library can be a rich source of marriages for men who were serving in the Army there or who were helping to run or develop that area of the British Empire. Many of our ancestors were posted there for a short period but, whilst there, they may have courted and married.

There are also marriages in the collection of non-statutory returns to be found in series RG 32–36 at the National Archives and the Family Records Centre. Indexed in RG 43/7–14, they date from as early as 1627. *Tracing Your Ancestors in the Public Record Office* by Amanda Bevan and *The British Overseas: A Guide to Records of Their Baptisms, Births, Marriages, Deaths and Burials Available in the United Kingdom* by Geoffrey Yeo list what records exist for places around the world where your British ancestors may have married.

The marriages of our ancestors, whilst living abroad for some reason, may be found in the International Memoranda at Guildhall Library in MS 10926/1–13, indexed on the open shelves (MS 10926C/1–2).

If not found in any of these sources, a marriage record may be located through the local or national system of registration pertaining to the country where the couple lived at that time. If this locality can be established, a copy of the document can be obtained. The date of commencement of registration and exactly what was recorded will vary considerably. Addresses and fees for searches and documents can be obtained through the *International Vital Records Handbook*.

Marriages before 1837

Prior to the introduction of civil registration on 1 July 1837, you will need to find the record of any marriage which took place in England and Wales in the register of a parish church or for a place of worship of another denomination.

Before 1754, a wide range of sects, in addition to the Church of England, performed ceremonies which resulted in the couple being declared husband and wife. Irregular and clandestine ceremonies were also performed. The couple may have jumped over a broomstick in a field or have married in an unregulated chapel or institution, such as the Fleet Prison or the Mayfair Chapel.

The records of the Fleet, which cover the period from 1667 to 1753, are to be found at the National Archives and the Family Records Centre in series RG 7. Only a few very small and selective indexes have been produced and published so far.

Hardwicke's Marriage Act of 1753 sought to regulate matrimony and prevent clandestine marriages. Not only did it seek to eliminate illicit marriage ceremonies, it also prevented unions in all nonconformist buildings, with the exception of Quakers and Jews. Those two religions already kept a very strict rein on their members.

Henceforth, all marriages were required to take place in the Church of England. This can often result in a separation in the records in which your family will be found. The baptisms of the children of a Congregationalist or even a Catholic, and perhaps their burials, will be found in a non-conformist register. The union of the parents will need to be sought in the register of a Church of England parish.

Marriage indexes

To locate a marriage, there are a number of finding aids and indexes. The International Genealogical Index and the British Isles Vital Records Index (2nd edition) are each very good initial sources for finding a missing union of ancestors.

In addition, there are many national and local marriage indexes. These should be consulted, depending on the geographical area and decade in which the marriage is most likely to have taken place. The index section of *The Phillimore Atlas & Index of Parish Registers* provides a pictorial guide to the index that provides the best chance of success.

Boyd's Marriage Index, compiled under the direction of Percival Boyd, may include marriages in the county that interests you. Divided into separate sections for men and women and produced as a typescript, it provides a very useful method of locating missing marriages. The marriages are arranged in 25-year periods, from 1538 to 1837. The first and last sections cover slightly longer periods. Some counties have their own index whilst others, with a smaller coverage, are included in the so-called Miscellaneous Series. Surnames are indexed phonetically to a certain extent, with similar names being grouped together. The original version of Boyd's Marriage Index is at the Society of Genealogists but has been made available on microfiche so it can be viewed in record offices and larger libraries. Most usefully, it is incorporated into the Origins database at *www.britishorigins.com*. This allows you to search a much wider geographical area more easily. Searches can be made for names that sound the same too. This cannot be done so easily in the original typescript format.

Pallot's Marriage Index was compiled in the 19th century and includes entries from 1780 to 1837. Produced from parish registers and augmented with printed material, especially from the printed *Phillimore Marriage Register* series from other counties of England, it contains nearly one million entries. The groom and bride are indexed separately on very thin pieces of tissue

Smart data: Boyd's indexes

The genealogist Percival Boyd (1866–1955) compiled important indexes of great value to the family historian. His **Marriage Index** is probably the most well known. It was made at his expense between 1925 and 1955, and has since been expanded. Though far from complete, it includes entries from the registers of about 4,300 English parishes as well as from marriage licences. Recording some 7 million brides and grooms, it is estimated to contain about 15 per cent of all marriages from 1538 to 1837.

Boyd also produced a **London Burial Index.** Concentrating on the area of the City of London, but including records from other parishes of the Greater London area from 1538 to 1853, over a quarter of a million entries can be searched.

Boyd's **Citizens of London,** compiled from many original and printed sources, brings together genealogical information about those who traded in the metropolis, mainly in the 16th and 17th centuries.

paper or card. Now the property of the Institute of Heraldic and Genealogical Studies, it can be searched for a fee. It has also been filmed by Ancestry.com and is available on compact disk and through their subscription website *www.ancestry.co.uk.* Unfortunately, the compilation of the computerized index by Ancestry leaves a great deal to be desired. The reading of the additional notes and parishes of residence of bride and groom is often very bizarre. It is imperative that you use the facility available on the site to examine the filmed image of the original slip. You can then decipher what the 19th-century indexer noted from the primary source. If it is still not legible, go back and examine the original church entry. You will probably need to do this anyway since usually only the year of the marriage is shown in the Pallot Index. The slip may not indicate whether the marriage was by banns or licence.

This marriage index provides an excellent way of finding marriages in the half-century just before the beginning of civil registration. It is especially good for marriages in what is now Greater London. It includes virtually all the marriages solemnized within the surviving registers of the 103 churches of the square mile of the City of London. It is also very good for those areas or parishes whose records are not included in the International Genealogical Index (produced by the Mormons). This is especially true of the East End of London around Wapping and the very large and popular parish of St Andrew, Holborn. Some of the parishes included had their records destroyed during the Blitz in World War II. In these cases, it is not possible to examine the register in which the marriage was originally found. At least the entry was indexed before the original was lost for ever. The Blitz itself also severely damaged the equivalent Pallot's Baptismal Index. Only about 100,000 slips survived.

Family history societies and individuals have compiled many local marriage indexes. These may cover a whole county or diocese for a specific time period. Alternatively, only a small group of parishes may have been indexed. Some are published or are available in record offices. Many others remain in private hands. In those cases, the compiler will conduct searches for a specific marriage. You can also obtain listings of all entries for a surname in a certain time period. All that is required is the payment of a small fee and a stamped self-addressed envelope. You can identify the index which will provide the best chance of success by consulting *Marriage and Census Indexes for Family Historians* by Jeremy Gibson and Elizabeth Hampson. The website *www.family historyonline.net* has brought together many of the indexes produced by family history societies and their members. You can then search them very inexpensively.

If all else fails, you may resort to searching systematically outwards, in all directions, from the place of baptism of the oldest known child. You can try the marriage registers of each church in turn in a suitable time frame. A much more sensible strategy is to make use of the records of how the marriage took place. These can allow the union to be found more easily.

Banns or licence?

A marriage can be solemnized after the calling of banns. If so, the intention to marry was read out in the parish churches of both bride and groom on three successive Sundays. This allowed parish-ioners in both localities to protest against the illegality of the marriage if any impediment was known. Importantly for us, the announcement of the proclamation was recorded in the banns book. This may be a separate volume or may be part of the marriage register itself. Dating from 1754 to 1837, the books are usually in the appro-priate county record office along with the more familiar baptism, marriage and burial records. They are a much under-used source. Even if the couple did not marry where the children were christened, the banns book can show the parish of residence of the other partner. This valuable clue may lead you to the church where their union took place.

On the other hand, your ancestors could have married after obtaining a licence. A wide range of ecclesiastical authorities, such as the Diocesan and Prerogative Courts, issued these. In general, the licence itself does not survive. It was taken by the couple to the chosen church to prove their entitlement to marry. The original document will eventually have been disposed of by a later incumbent as being no longer worth keeping. Some have been saved. The very large collection of original licences made by Crisp from London churches for the 18th and 19th centuries was dispersed. The Institute of Heraldic and Genealogical Studies in Canterbury maintains the largest section. Other volumes are at the Society of Genealogists or are in private hands. Abstracts of the collection and an index to the surnames included were compiled and can be used at the Society of Genealogists.

When the licence was obtained, two other documents were produced. These are very important in research. The marriage allegation records the ages, marital status and parish of residence of groom and bride. It is unusual to obtain a statement of age from other marriage documentation. It is unlikely to be recorded in the parish register. Often only the statement 'of 21 years and upwards' is recorded. If so, this means that the couple were 'of full age' and did not need parental permission to wed. If an exact age was stated, the allegation can prove invaluable in eliminating some candidates for the baptism of the man or woman. Some would have been much older or younger than the couple who married. Thus, they are unlikely to have been your ancestors. Without such clues, the wrong person could be chosen.

The occupation of the groom may be stated. From that, you may be able to identify the marriage of a man with a very common combination of names to the exclusion of other men who had married women with the same forename. Most importantly, if the place of marriage is not yet known, the allegation shows one or more churches where the wedding could occur. It must be stressed that the application for a licence does not necessarily mean that the marriage ceremony ever took place.

A bond was issued to try to ensure that it did, and a fine would be exacted if the wedding did not take place. The marriage bond may also record the occupation and current marital status of the groom. Information about a bondsman is given. He may have been a relative to the groom.

These documents will be found in the diocesan archive. This will be the same office where the bishops' transcripts and probate material for that area are stored. *Bishops' Transcripts and Marriage Licences, Bonds and Allegations* by Jeremy Gibson provides you with information about the survival of this material in each area. Indexes and finding aids are listed.

Many lists and indexes to licences, bonds and allegations are published. The Society of Genealogists has a very large collection of these, including copies of the calendars to the records from the relevant record office. These can be found through the Index to County Sources section of the catalogue, which is online at *www.sog.org. uk/sogcat/access/*.

Two major courts had the authority to issue allegations, bonds and licences. These were the Faculty Office and the Vicar General of the Archbishop of Canterbury. They were both important where the bride and groom lived in different dioceses or even archdioceses. Inhabitants of London frequently used them. So did couples from all over England and Wales. The original records are at Lambeth Palace Library but the allegations to as late as 1851 can be used on microfilm at the Society of Genealogists.

Both sets are indexed on *www.britishorigins.com*. The index to the Faculty Office records shows both forename and surname, whilst that for the Vicar General records is much more basic, providing only the surnames for the happy couple. The index to the allegations issued by the Vicar General can also be searched at the Family Records Centre.

Whichever ecclesiastical authority issued the licence, its indexes can provide an invaluable means of locating a missing marriage.

Divorce

Some marriages inevitably ended in divorce. Legal termination of marriage was very rare before 1858 and could only be achieved through Act of Parliament. These Acts are held at the House of Lords Record Office. Annulment could also be obtained through an ecclesiastical court (*see* Chapter 5).

Divorce records from 1858 are at the Principal Registry of the Family Division in High Holborn, London. These are not open to the public. A search can be paid for and, if successful, a copy of the Decree Absolute obtained. The indexes are available for research on microfilm in J 78 at the Family Records Centre or at the National Archives from 1858 to 1958.

The surviving divorce files for 1858 to 1938 are also available in series J 77. A very small sample of later files has also been kept. All surviving files from 1858 to 2002, which are kept at the National Archives, are searchable through *www.nationalarchives.gov.uk/catalogue.*

Census returns

Your ancestors should be found in a decennial census if they were alive at any time from 1841 to 1901. This is an essential tool for research. From 1851, the returns record the vital piece of information about where and when the person believed that they had been born. If accurate, they can lead us to the birth or baptism of the person under investigation (*see* Chapter 1). Such statements may vary considerably about the same person in different enumerations.

The returns for 1841 will only point us in the direction of an area, such as the same county, the rest of England or Wales, Scotland, Ireland or 'Foreign Parts'. Do not forget that ages for adults in this first national listing might be rounded down to the nearest five-year interval. Thus

someone said to be 65 could be anywhere between 65 and 69 years of age. Most importantly,
relationships were not recorded. One can often
only infer the interconnection between those in
the same household, based on their ages.

Census indexes

Many censuses have now been indexed by
surname. You should search any national or local
surname index.

The six censuses from 1851 to 1901 are completely indexed by name and can be searched at
www.ancestry.co.uk. You will need to have taken
out a subscription to use these at home. All,
except 1901, can be searched free of charge at
the Family Records Centre or the National
Archives. All six indexes are free to those who
use the library at the Society of Genealogists.
The search can be limited to a particular county
or place of residence or birthplace if the name
is common. By using wildcard searches, you can
look for spelling variants or misindexing.

You can view the original image online. Before
doing that, though, it is often useful to use the
option to view, in transcript form, those who are
on the same page or the other family members in
the same household. You can then select the

right family. The page can then be printed out on-line, if you have good print facilities. If not, note the reference and obtain a better-quality copy from the microfilm copy at the National Archives, the Family Records Centre or a local record office or library.

The National Archives' own pay-for-view version of the index to the 1901 census is *www.1901censusonline.com*. All the normal search criteria can be used to locate the person you seek.

An alternative free version of the 1881 census can be searched at *www.familysearch.org* or *www.familyhistoryonline.net*. This index, produced as a joint venture by the Church of Jesus Christ of Latter-day Saints and the Federation of Family History Societies, is also available on CD-ROM; the set of disks can be purchased. In both cases you can search by age, county of residence or birth. A microfiche version of the index can also be used. This can be searched nationally or by county. It is useful if you wish to print out a list of anyone with a certain name in a particular area.

A pay-for-view index to the 1861 census is also being produced by *www.1837online.com*, and *www.britishorigins.com* is working on indexes to the 1841 and 1871 census.

Where two versions of a national index exist and you cannot find the family or person in one, try the other. The indexes will be very different!

The returns of 1851 for the counties of Warwickshire, Devon and Norfolk were indexed by the Church of Jesus Christ of Latter-day Saints and the Federation of Family History Societies as a pilot project for the national index to the 1881 census. It is produced on CD-ROM and on microfiche.

Many local indexes to those who lived in a parish, a registration district or a county were produced before the national indexes became available. The 1851 census was often indexed first as it was the first enumeration which recorded place of birth. These local indexes still have their use and you should not ignore them just because there is now a national finding aid. If you cannot find your person in the 'easy to use' online indexes, go back to any other available index.

Where an index has been compiled for a geographical area from 1841 to 1901, it may have been published in a range of different media or remain in private hands. Some are full indexes and transcripts, some are indexes to the full names of all individuals whilst others just list the piece and folio number on which people with a particular surname can be found and viewed. Most will be available at the Family Records Centre or Society of Genealogists. Many can be used locally in the record offices and libraries for the area concerned. A guide to the whereabouts of many indexes, especially those which are unpublished and remain with the compiler, can be found in *Marriage and Census Indexes for Family Historians* compiled by Jeremy Gibson and Elizabeth Hampson. Some are available at a very reasonable fee at *www.familyhistory.net* or can be searched free through *http://freecen. rootsweb.com*.

All are very useful for tracking down a very mobile ancestor or relative who, for some reason, was away on the night of the census. You may have an ancestor who was in service, had joined the forces or was in apprenticeship. He could have left to seek his fortune and may have taken a position many miles from his native place, or she may have been a married woman who had gone to live in her husband's home parish.

Original returns

If you still think that a person lived in a particular place at a certain time, be prepared to ignore the lack of a suitable entry in an index and search the original returns anyway. You may be surprised to find that the person is recorded with a variant spelling of the surname, which you had not thought of so far. The name may have been completely misread by whoever compiled the name index.

Censuses can be searched nationally at the National Archives or the Family Records Centre or locally in record offices or libraries. Many researchers are prepared to search page by page through the returns of a large area looking for a missing person.

Others use an address found in another source that they have examined. Birth, marriage or death certificates, commercial or trade directories (Chapter 6), newspapers, service or occupational records (Chapters 4 and 6), wills or obituaries (Chapter 7) are the most useful for providing addresses. Any other document or source that provides an address or even a parish or town of residence for an ancestor in association with a date or time period is a useful clue to finding them in a census.

Many census returns have been published or made available to the researcher on microfiche, in booklets or on CD-ROM. These may be found in record offices and libraries or are available for purchase through commercial organizations or family history societies. Some have indexes attached to them. Whatever the method, you must take all steps to find your ancestor in a census.

Smart reading on marriage records

Bishops' Transcripts and Marriage Licences, Bonds and Allegations, by Jeremy Gibson, 5th edn (Federation of Family History Societies, 2001)

The British Overseas: A Guide to Records of Their Baptisms, Births, Marriages, Deaths and Burials Available in the United Kingdom, by Geoffrey Yeo, revised by Philippa Smith, 3rd edn (Guildhall Library, 1994)

International Vital Records Handbook, 4th edn (Genealogical Publishing, 2000)

Marriage and Census Indexes for Family Historians, by Jeremy Gibson and Elizabeth Hampson, 8th edn (Federation of Family History Societies, 2000)

The Phillimore Atlas & Index of Parish Registers, by C.R. Humphery-Smith, 3rd edn (Phillimore, 2003)

Tracing Your Ancestors in the Public Record Office, by Amanda Bevan, 6th edn (Public Record Office, 2002); 7th edition, forthcoming (the National Archives, 2006)

Chapter 4

The fighting man

- The Army
- Soldiers
- Army officers
- World War I
- The Royal Air Force
- The Royal Navy
- Naval officers
- The Royal Marines
- Marine officers
- Militia and yeomanry

All of us must have an ancestor who served in one of the armed services. Such men may have been career soldiers or sailors, or they could have been among the millions who joined up to serve Crown and country during one of the wars fought by the British over the past four centuries. Those engaged in defending the nation against an enemy or policing the British Empire moved from country to country.

Tracing the life and service of a fighting man can be very rewarding and very taxing at the same time. It may be difficult to track them down in a census to discover a place of birth. They often seem to have been out of the country at the time that they should have been recorded, and only the wife and children were left behind to provide genealogical information about them. However, we can learn in which acts of history our ancestor was involved by discovering the names of the regiment and campaigns he fought in, or on which ships or in which squadron he served. We can find out exactly what he was doing on a certain day. This is true of very few of our ancestors.

It is impossible to include here all the sources available for research into a fighting forebear. However, the important tool for research is to know how to begin the process. This will depend on the part of the armed forces that your man served in, whether he was an officer or in the ranks, and the conflicts in which he was active. Once you have made the initial step, there are many detailed guidebooks that will help you to go further.

To expand your search, you will probably have to visit a national service museum. A specialist regimental museum may also hold other material relevant to your research. These can be found in *A Guide to Military Museums and Other Places of Military Interest* by T. and S. Wise. You should also read a regimental history or diary to put your soldier into the context of his campaigns.

Find out whether anyone has already compiled an index to the type of serviceman your ancestor was, or to the records of a conflict in which he might have served. *Specialist Indexes for Family Historians* by Jeremy Gibson and Elizabeth Hampson includes a number of very useful indexes to those who were in the armed services.

If we must begin original research, how do we start?

The Army

It is generally easier to trace the career of an officer rather than an ordinary soldier. Those who gave the orders usually stayed in the Army for longer than those who joined for a limited period of service in the ranks. For the period from the 17th century to the end of World War I, a wealth of information is available, mostly at the National Archives. Records are only open for research for soldiers who served until about 1920. After that, the records are closed but can be searched and copied for a fee for the next of kin, or others identified as having their consent, by the Ministry of Defence.

Soldiers

To trace the records of a non-commissioned officer or enlisted man who survived his period of service and applied for a pension, the usual starting point is series WO 97 at the National Archives. These are the Attestation and Discharge Papers usually referred to as 'Soldiers' Documents'. They are easy to access for 1760 to 1854 and from 1883 to the beginning of World War I.

The names of those in the first period are included in the National Archives catalogue *www. nationalarchives.gov.uk/catalogue*. This will allow the original documents to be found. They are on microfilm and so are available through family history centres (Church of Jesus Christ of Latter-day

Saints) as well as at the National Archives, and copies are at the Society of Genealogists. For the soldiers of the second period, the records are in two alphabetical series, one for 1883–1900 and the other for 1900–13 (dates of discharge), irrespective of the regiment in which the man served. It is very easy to see whether your soldier is included in either. If so, you can copy his records.

The problem is the intervening period of 1855 to 1882. If he was discharged from 1873 to 1882, you need to know what type of soldier he was. Even if you don't know that, there are only four separate indexes to search. These are for men who were in the cavalry, artillery, infantry or corps.

From 1855 to 1872, as the records are arranged by the name of the regiment, you need to know that information for your soldier. This can be discovered in a number of ways.

You can learn this vital piece of information from a marriage or death certificate for the soldier himself or from a birth, marriage or death certificate for one of his children. These are found in the records of civil registration of the country where he served, from the separate Miscellaneous Section at the Family Records Centre, which includes Army records, and, of course, from the extensive collection of material for those who served on the Indian sub-continent, which is held at the British Library (*see* Chapters 1, 3 and 7).

The name of his regiment may be determined by finding him or his family in a census or from information recorded in a will. There may be service documents, such as a pay book, for him in family papers. You, or an expert, may identify his uniform from a photograph or painting.

If you know where your man was serving at a particular time, the Monthly Returns show where each regiment was stationed in a given month. These are in WO 17 and 73. Thankfully, J.M. Kitzmiller lists which regiments were where during each campaign in his book *In Search of the 'Forlorn Hope': A Comprehensive Guide to Locating British Regiments and Their Records*. This can dramatically limit the number of regiments that you must search.

If your soldier received a pension, this was paid by the district office where he lived. If you know where he settled after leaving the Army, his record can be found. It will only note any change in payment. This will be when he was first paid his pension, when he moved district, when there was a change in the size of the pension and, of course, when he died. The records are in the District Pension Returns, WO 22. They date from

1842 to 1883 and the name of the regiment was included.

Once you have found his papers in WO 97, they will give you great detail about him, including his place of birth, age or birth date, his place of enlistment, previous trade, full physical description and distinguishing marks. There may be a complete medical history. You will learn about his misdemeanours and medals, details of his family and next of kin, when and where he was discharged and where he may have gone to live.

A great deal can be learned about his career and life in the Army by tracking him through the musters and pay lists in WO 10–16 to 1898 and through the description books and records of deserters in WO 25 and 67. The musters are the lists of soldiers who were serving in a given unit, such as a battalion of a regiment, in a particular month; thus there were 12 musters a year. There are also pension records and even information about those who were tried by court martial. Some pension material, such as that in WO 121 for 1787 to 1813, can be searched at *www.nationalarchives.gov.uk/catalogue*.

For those who died in service and did not receive a pension, a record should be found in the various records of death for soldiers discussed in Chapter 7. Otherwise, you should look in the casualty returns or payments to next of kin, which are in WO 25.

Army officers

It is generally much easier to trace the career of an officer. A summary of his life can be tracked through the *Army Lists* published from the mid-18th century. These show the dates of commissions and promotions. They detail the campaigns in which he fought, the medals he won and his notable actions in battle. The officers are listed by regiment and then by rank. There is an alphabetical index of all officers in each volume. Disappearance from the listings or a statement that he had become non-active or was on half-pay is often significant. Promotions, casualties, the award of medals and heroic feats in battle were also recorded in the *London Gazette*. Those listed in citations in the 20th century can be searched at *www.gazettes-online.co.uk*. Once the date of a commission has been established, further information about the appointment can be located in the Commander-in-Chief's Memoranda Papers from 1793 to 1870 in WO 31.

The main series of original records for officers' service are WO 25 and 76. These date from as early as 1764, but the bulk of the records are from the early 19th century. They provide a retrospective synopsis of his career, his commissions and campaigns. They show his date and place of birth and often information about his marriage and children. There may also be certificates and church entries of baptism, marriage and burial for him. They are in WO 42. Pensions records of officers and their widows for the 18th and 19th centuries are in WO 23–25 and in the records of the Paymaster General.

To learn more about tracing the history of a soldier or officer, consult S. Fowler and W. Spencer, *Army Records for Family Historians*, or *My Ancestor Was in the British Army: How Can I Find Out More about Him?* by M.J. Watts and C. Watts.

World War I

If your ancestor was one of the more than seven million men (and some women) who served in the Great War, it should be possible to find out more about him or her. *Army Service Records of the First World War* by W. Spencer is a research guide to the records of that conflict.

Although many of the records were destroyed or badly damaged during the Blitz, much has survived or been reconstructed, conserved and

Smart data: Diaries of World War I
Official war diaries were kept for each battalion by junior officers, and may now be found at the National Archives in Kew with, sometimes, an additional copy at regimental headquarters. While they rarely mention individual servicemen by name, the wealth of official details they offer about daily life and operations can help fill in the picture of your ancestor's World War I experience or help you to confirm a date or particular event. It should be remembered that these are official diaries; a collection of personal diaries of war that have come into public hands is kept by the Imperial War Museum in London.

microfilmed in WO 363 and 364. They include records of soldiers who were discharged or who died between 1914 and 1920. These may have been men who had been in the Army long before World War I started. The records do not include officers or those who continued to serve after 1920. Both alphabetical series should be searched. If successful, the information will be very similar to that recorded in the Attestation and Discharge Papers of WO 97. If no trace is found in either set of service records, you should search the medal rolls of WO 372. The filmed cards are indexed alphabetically. They are now searchable online at *www.nationalarchives. gov. uk/documentsonline/medals.asp* and should allow his regiment and service number to be determined.

The equivalent service records of Army officers in the World War I were mostly destroyed in the bombing during the World War II. Some survived and are in WO 339 and 374. These are accessed through WO 338. Those names which appear in WO 339 can be searched through the National Archives online catalogue *www. nationalarchives.gov.uk/catalogue.*

Further information about any World War I soldier who died in action can be found through the Commonwealth War Graves Commission at *www.cwgc.org. Soldiers Died in the Great War* (Naval and Military Press) is a CD-ROM index and database for both officers and other soldiers. *The Roll of Honour: A Biographical Record of Members of His Majesty's Naval and Military Forces Who Fell in the Great War 1914–1918* by the Marquis de Ruvigny lists some of those who died, providing a photograph and some genealogical information.

The National Roll of the Great War 1914– 1918 details, in 14 geographical volumes, some

150,000 men, both survivors and those who died. The information was supplied by the men them- selves if they had survived, or by their families. Some volumes are published on CD-ROM.

The Royal Air Force

From 1914 to March 1918, the records of service for those of the non-commissioned ranks who served in the Royal Flying Corps are included in WO 363 and 364. The records of ratings who were in the Royal Naval Air Service are included with those who were in the Royal Navy in ADM 188. Royal Naval Air Service officers can be found in ADM 273. Records of officers of the Royal Flying Corps who ceased their service before the formation of the Royal Air Force are in WO 339 and 374.

The records of both ranks and officers from 1918, when the Royal Air Force was formed, are to be found in AIR 76, 78 and 79 at the National Archives. Most service records for those who continued to serve after 1920, including in World War II, are still held by the Ministry of Defence and can only be searched for by next of kin.

The many who were killed in action, especially from 1939 to 1945, are recorded in the Miscel- laneous Section of the Family Records Centre (*see* Chapter 7) and by the Commonwealth War Graves Commission.

William Spencer's *Air Force Records for Family Historians* or E. Wilson's *The Records of the Royal Air Force: How to Find the Few* will lead you to other sources for those who served in this branch of the services.

The Royal Navy

From 1853 to 1923, it should be quite straight-forward to trace the service record of an ordinary naval seaman. His Service Number and Continuous Service Record will enable his career to be researched. ADM 139, for those entering from 1853 to 1872, and ADM 188, for 1873 to 1923, should be searched at the National Archives. The records will include his date and place of birth, date of engagement, physical description, the names of the ships on which he served and what happened to him at the end of his time in the Navy. For those who served after 1923, the records are still held by the Ministry of Defence, to which application should be made.

For dates before 1853, you must know the name of the ship on which a man was serving for a particular voyage before his records can be found. As with soldiers, this may be identified from a certificate of marriage or death for the sailor or a similar document for one of his children. Parish register entries, census returns, wills or photographs may also help with finding the name of a ship whose records can then be searched.

If the sailor was paid a pension in the 19th century, you will be able to find out the names of the ships on which he served through ADM 29 or 73. The first of these series can now be searched online at *www.nationalarchives. gov.uk/catalogue.*

Once the names of his ships are known, together with the dates on which he was on board, a more in-depth study of his time in the Navy can be pursued through the ships' musters in ADM 36–39 and 41 or the ships' pay books in ADM 31–35 for 1667 to 1878. Medal rolls for 1793 to 1972 in ADM 171 and pension records in ADM 6, ADM 22 and WO 22 can add to our knowledge. Those who were tried for misconduct can be traced from 1680 to 1965 in ADM 1 and 156. Seamen's wills for 1786 to 1882 are in ADM 48 and 44.

Many other personnel were employed by the Navy, not on board ships but in naval dockyards. A wealth of records exists for them and their families too.

Naval officers

The careers of naval officers can be tracked through the *Navy Lists* which date from 1782. Notable events in the lives of such men, including their commissions, promotions and deaths, were published by the *London Gazette*.

Much of this information, together with other genealogical and historical information, is collected in *The Commissioned Sea Officers of the Royal Navy 1660–1815* by D. Syrett and R.L. DiNardo. W.R. O'Byrne's *A Naval Biographical Dictionary: Comprising the Life and Services of Every Living Officer in Her Majesty's Navy, from the Rank of Admiral of the Fleet to that of Lieutenant* listed all those, from the rank of lieutenant and upward, who were alive in 1845. J. Marshall, in his *Royal Naval Biography, or Memoirs of the Services of All the Flag-Officers, Captains and Commanders whose Names Appeared on the Admiralty List of Sea Officers at the Commencement of the Present Year [1823], or who have since been promoted*, printed biographies of those who were of at least the rank of commander or captain by the late 18th and early 19th centuries. Between them, these three sources provide a good chance of finding an account of the life of an officer before 1845.

Consolidated Registers of Officers' Services were maintained from 1756 to 1966 in ADM 196. These include names of the ships on which the officer served, his appointments and genealogical information about him and his family. It is most complete for 1840 to 1920. Surveys of the careers of officers were taken in 1817 and 1846. These can be found in ADM 9 and 10.

In order to pass through the commissioned ranks, officers were required to be successful in examinations. Those for lieutenants are in ADM 6, 13 and 107. The names included are indexed in B. Pappalardo's *Royal Navy Lieutenants' Passing Certificates, 1691–1902.*

Many other types of warrant officer, such as carpenters, gunners and masters, also have passing certificates in ADM 6, 13 and 106. There are name indexes to some series.

Officers were, of course, recorded on the musters of their ship, just like the men. Other records can also be found. The grant of an officer's pension or an application from his destitute widow, naming her dependents, may be found in many series of the Admiralty or the Paymaster General. Many claims were supported by other genealogical documents. His will, if proved from 1830 to 1860, may be found in ADM 45.

To learn more about naval records, read *Tracing Your Naval Ancestors* by Bruno Pappalardo.

The Royal Marines

To locate the service records of a Marine, it is necessary to know the Division in which he served. There were four of these: Chatham, Plymouth, Portsmouth and, from 1805 to 1869, Woolwich. Attestation Forms, completed by recruits on joining the service and dating from 1790 into the 20th century, are in ADM 157. These show age or date and place of birth, previous occupation and physical description, and give a record of his service. The Description Books can be used to back these up from as early as 1755 to as late as 1940 in ADM 158. Full records of service from 1842 to 1946 are found in ADM 159 and are indexed in ADM 313.

Marine officers

Marine officers can be found in *Army Lists* or *Navy Lists*. Their detailed service records are in class ADM 196 from 1793 to 1925, usually giving the name and occupation of their father. They are fully indexed.

Pension records for all Marines can be searched in ADM 165 and 166 and their medals are included with those of the Royal Navy in ADM 171.

For those who attested after 1925, records are still held by the Ministry of Defence to whom application can be made. Next of kin can obtain copies of surviving records.

Other records of those who were in the Marines are described in *Records of the Royal Marines* by G. Thomas.

Militia and yeomanry

Your ancestor may have been a man who was ready to be called up on the threat of invasion or civil unrest. If so, he may be found in the records of those who were members of the various county militia regiments, yeomanries and sea fencibles (a naval reserve force raised for home defence against Napoleon).

These sources for the earlier years are normally to be found in a county record office. The surviving list can be found through Jeremy Gibson and Alan Dell's *Tudor and Stuart Muster Rolls: A Directory of Holdings in the British Isles*. Later records may still be held locally or are deposited at the National Archives. *Militia Lists and Musters 1757–1876: A Directory of Holdings in the British Isles* by Jeremy Gibson and Mervyn Medlycott deals with those of the 18th and 19th centuries. Militia lists show eligible men, not just those who served.

WO 68 (1759–1925) contains the service records for militia regiments, both officers and other ranks. Some genealogical evidence for militiamen and their families, together with information on casualties and misbehaviour, is to be found there. You may even find a physical description of your ancestor.

Attestation Papers for 1769 to 1915 are in WO 96 and 97. They often include date and place of birth. The Muster Books are in class WO 13 (1780–1878). Pensions are recorded from 1817 to the early 20th century in PMG 13 and WO 116. To discover more about those who served here, consult *Records of the Militia and Volunteer Forces 1757–1945* by William Spencer.

Smart reading on military records

Air Force Records for Family Historians, by William Spencer (Public Record Office, 2000)

Army Records for Family Historians, by S. Fowler and W. Spencer, 2nd edn (Public Record Office, 1998, reprinted 2000)

Army Service Records of the First World War, by W. Spencer, 3rd edn (Public Record Office, 2001)

The Commissioned Sea Officers of the Royal Navy 1660–1815, by D. Syrett and R.L. DiNardo (Naval Records Society, 1994)

A Guide to Military Museums and Other Places of Military Interest, by T. and S. Wise, 10th edn (T. Wise, 2001)

In Search of the 'Forlorn Hope': A Comprehensive Guide to Locating British Regiments and Their Records, by J.M. Kitzmiller (Manuscript Publishing Foundation, 1988)

Militia Lists and Musters 1757–1876: A Directory of Holdings in the British Isles, by Jeremy Gibson and Mervyn Medlycott, 4th edn (Federation of Family History Societies, 2000)

My Ancestor Was in the British Army: How Can I Find Out More about Him?, by M.J. Watts and C. Watts (Society of Genealogists, 1995)

The National Roll of the Great War 1914–1918 (National Publishing Company, 1918–1922), 14 vols

A Naval Biographical Dictionary; Comprising the Life and Services of Every Living Officer in Her Majesty's Navy, from the Rank of Admiral of the Fleet to that of Lieutenant, by W.R. O'Byrne (John Murray, 1849)

Records of the Militia and Volunteer Forces 1757–1945, by W. Spencer (Public Record Office, 1997)

The Records of the Royal Air Force: How to Find the Few, by E. Wilson (Federation of Family History Societies, 1991)

Records of the Royal Marines, by G. Thomas (Public Record Office, 1994)

The Roll of Honour: A Biographical Record of Members of His Majesty's Naval and Military Forces Who Fell in the Great War 1914–1918, by Marquis de Ruvigny (reprint, London School of Economics, 1987)

Royal Naval Biography, or Memoirs of the Services of All the Flag-officers, Captains and Commanders whose Names Appeared on the Admiralty List of Sea Officers at the Commencement of the Present Year [1823], or who have since been promoted, by J. Marshall (Longman, Hurst, Rees, Orme and Brown, 1823–35)

Royal Navy Lieutenants' Passing Certificates, 1691–1902, by B. Pappalardo (List and Index Society, vols 289–90, 2001)

Specialist Indexes for Family Historians, by Jeremy Gibson and Elizabeth Hampson, 2nd edn (Federation of Family History Societies, 2000)

Tracing Your Naval Ancestors, by Bruno Pappalardo (Public Record Office, 2003)

Tudor and Stuart Muster Rolls: A Directory of Holdings in the British Isles, by Jeremy Gibson and Alan Dell (Federation of Family History Societies, 1991)

FOR KING AND COUNTRY: OFFICERS ON THE ROLL OF HONOUR.

PHOTOGRAPHS BY BASSANO, RUSSELL, VANDYK, TOPICAL, WESTON, ELLIS AND WALERY, GWEN GIBBS, ELLIOTT AND FRY, LAFAYETTE, AND GOVERS.

CAPT. EVELYN S. MARSHALL, Royal Warwickshire Regiment. Son of Canon E. T. Marshall, Sutton Vicarage, Cambridgeshire. Died of wounds.

CAPT. ROY MOLYNEUX QUILTER, Bedfordshire Regiment. Son of late Mr. John S. Quilter, F.R.I.B.A., and Mrs. Quilter, of Streatham.

LIEUT. R. H. DAY, Royal Warwickshire Regt. Received commission June 1915, and was recently promoted. Killed in action.

CAPT. ALAN J. BOWLES, Royal Berkshire Regt. Only son of Captain F. A. R. Bowles, R.N., and of Mrs. Bowles.

CAPT. A. W. GALE, D.S.O., 2nd Life Guards. Son of Mr. A. C. Gale, of St. Cross, Winchester. Was awarded the D.S.O. in March.

CAPT. GEOFFREY WOODHAMS, Royal Sussex Regt. Son of Mr. Alfred Woodhams, Littlehampton. Killed while rescuing a wounded soldier.

MAJOR NEVILLE S. MANN, L. North Lancashire Regt. Had been A.D.C. to the Governor and Commander-in-Chief of the Leeward Islands.

CAPT. T. C. M. AUSTIN, S. Wales Borderers. Son of Rev. and Mrs. A. D. Austin, Upper Norwood. Was mentioned in Sir Ian Hamilton's despatch.

CAPT. D. W. G. JACKSON, R. Welsh Fusiliers. Eldest son of Rev. and Mrs. G. H. Jackson, Hasfield Rectory, Glos.

CAPT. ERIC C. SCHOOLING, R. Warwick. Regt. Son of Mr. Schooling, Bromley. Missing; now believed killed.

CAPT. R. NIGEL G. BARTLETT, E. Lancashire Regiment. Son of Rev. C. Oldfed Bartlett and Mrs. Bartlett, Minsterworth Vicarage, Gloucester.

LIEUT. VISCOUNT QUENINGTON, Gloucestershire Hussars Yeomanry. Eldest son of Earl St. Aldwyn. Viscountess Quenington died in March.

CAPT. NIGEL J. L. WICKHAM, Connaught Rangers. Son of the late Mr. Frederic Robert Wickham and Mrs. Wickham, Sea Point Lodge, Broadstairs.

2ND LIEUT. RONALD B. LOWE, Lincolnshire Regt. Youngest son of Mr. W. J. Lowe, of Westbury, Wilts. Aged 23.

2ND LIEUT. M. E. KING, Middlesex Regt. Son of late Mr. H. W. King, M.D., of Chester, and Mrs. King, Northwood.

LIEUT. O. A. MANN, Royal Lancaster Regt. Officially reported by the War Office killed in action.

2ND LT. W. H. DUCKWORTH, Lancashire Fusiliers. Eldest son of Mr. and Mrs. W. H. Duckworth, of Upper Gloucester Place.

LIEUT. CYRIL CHARLES HENRY, Worcestershire Regiment. Reported missing; now to have been killed. Son of Sir Charles S. Henry, M.P.

Chapter 5

Courts and criminals

- The courts
- Quarter Sessions
- The Assizes
- Gaol records
- Transportation
- The manorial court
- The equity courts
- The parish
- The ecclesiastical court

Our ancestors were subject to the laws of the land and of the community in which they lived. Today there is one main law enforcement agency that governs the police and court system. If anyone breaks the statutes laid down by Parliament, he or she will be dealt with by a system of judicial authorities. If the person is guilty, this will result either in a fine, payment of compensation or a term of imprisonment. A criminal record will ensue. This will be something for the descendants to use to find out about the person when such records are released for the scrutiny of the genealogists of the future.

The 16th to 19th centuries experienced a much more complex and all-pervading system of justice, which governed almost every aspect of daily life. Many different rules for moral, spiritual and behavioural well-being were laid down and enforced by many different types of court. Besides setting the laws and lores that our forebears were expected to live by, they required oaths to be sworn and taxes to be collected. Most people would have fallen foul of one of these authorities or have been recorded as paying or avoiding a tax or oath at one time or another. Even a common labourer, who apparently achieved little in life except to be baptized, marry, christen his own children and, eventually, be buried, might appear in these records. With luck, their existence may be brought to life, if only briefly, through the documentation produced by such courts.

The courts

The authorities which governed the day-to-day and long-term lives of our ancestors were:
- criminal courts: Quarter Sessions and Assizes;
- manorial courts;
- equity courts: Chancery, Exchequer, Star Chamber, Requests;
- ecclesiastical courts.

These courts might have recorded the process of one particular misdemeanour because it came under each of their jurisdictions. For example, a woman who gave birth to an illegitimate child could be arraigned before the ecclesiastical court for her lack of morals, and by the Quarter Sessions through the Poor Law for producing a child likely to become a drain on that community and to ensure that the reputed father assisted with its maintenance. If this all became too much for the unfortunate mother and she did away with her child, she could be tried for murder at the Assizes!

If additional clues are needed to flesh out the life of an ancestor, they may be found in these legal records. Many have good indexes or finding aids. Others require systematic searching, usually based on a lead from another, more usual, source. They can provide that vital breakthrough or lead you to a fascinating episode in the life of one of your ancestors.

Quarter Sessions

Many ancestors at some time would have attended this type of court. They might have been indicted to appear to answer for a misdemeanour that they were accused of committing. Alternatively, they could have been a witness at the hearing because they were the victim or had valuable evidence about the supposed crime. The scope of this court's jurisdiction was surprisingly large. Anything from the theft of a handkerchief to murder could be heard here. The more serious offences would be passed on to the Assize courts for further proceedings.

The records, covering the 14th century to 1971, are unlikely to provide a huge amount of genealogical information, although ages, occupations and parishes of residence can be discovered. However, the circumstances behind an alleged crime and the statements from the deponents or witnesses will be of great interest. The fate of the accused, through the sentence passed, may give the reason why the death or burial of an ancestor was not to be found in this country. The convicted person might have ended his days in one of the colonies to which convicts were transported. Many became inhabitants of our penal settlements in America, Australia and the West Indies.

The Quarter Sessions court did not just deal with criminal offences. It was responsible for licensing certain groups such as alehouse keepers, gamekeepers and higglers, hucksters and badgers (itinerant tradesmen). It even recorded nonconformists living in a particular area. These people may be completely absent from the parish records, but their appearance in the Sessions records confirms that they were living in the parish at a given time.

The maintenance of highways and turnpikes, gaols and sewers also came under the Sessions' authority. Reference to other individuals will be found in the documentation relating to the collection of taxes and the issuing of orders. The Hearth Tax (1662–89) was one levy in which the Quarter Sessions played an important role (*see* Chapter 6).

Smart data: Criminal courts

The **Quarter Sessions** were county courts that sat four times a year at Epiphany, Easter, Midsummer and Michaelmas, each session completing its proceedings in one day. Besides dealing with many civil matters, including licensing of tradesmen and the maintenance of public services, Justices of the Peace (magistrates) dealt with a wide range of crimes. They could pass severe sentences, including transportation, even for minor offences. More serious charges were usually heard by the **Assizes,** where judges and juries decided the outcome of the trial based on the evidence presented by witnesses. The courts travelled to each market town within a geographical division of the country, and the circuit could take anything from two to five weeks to complete. In 1971, both courts were replaced by Crown courts.

The Quarter Sessions also recorded, in brief, the disputes between parishes over the settlement rights of their inhabitants. So if the original Poor Law document has been lost through the clearance of the parish chest, a reference to its original existence and the bare bones of its content and substance can be traced (*see* page 155).

Most records are now found in the relevant county record office. For a guide to the records and indexes to the local material, see Jeremy Gibson's *Quarter Sessions Records for Family Historians: A Select List.*

A personal name index may have been produced for individuals who appear in a particular group, for instance nonconformists or gamekeepers, of the proceedings of the Quarter Sessions over a certain period of time. This may be searched in the county record office itself or may be in private hands. For such valuable shortcuts see *Specialist Indexes for Family Historians* by Jeremy Gibson. Access to Archives at *www.a2a. org.uk* often catalogues the names in Quarter Sessions records in many different repositories.

The Assizes

More serious offences were tried at more senior courts. Dating from as early as the 13th century to as late as 1971, their records are principally at the National Archives. The records of each county are found within the relevant circuits in series JUST and ASSI. There were special areas with individual jurisdiction before the 19th century, namely the Palatinates of Durham (records in class DURH) and Chester (designated as CHES at the National Archives). There were also separate courts for Wales and London. For Wales, the records are held at the National Library of Wales and date from 1532 to 1830.

London was a law unto itself. Before 1835, the main court was at the Old Bailey. This had jurisdiction over London and other parts of the Home Counties. The records for the City of London are held at Guildhall Library, whilst those for the other areas are to be found at the London Metropolitan Archives. The proceedings were reported in the *Old Bailey Sessions Papers*. These have now been made available from 1674 to 1834 through *www.oldbaileyonline.org*. This allows the synopsis of the trial, including detailed evidence given by witnesses, to be read.

From 1834, the Old Bailey was replaced by the Central Criminal Court, which sat at the same place. Its records are at the National Archives in class CRIM. The *Old Bailey Sessions Papers* continued to report its hearings until 1913. These are being included in a microfiche publication, *British Trials 1660–1900*, by Chadwyck Healey.

In general, the indictment should record the name of the prisoner, the crime, where he or she lived and perhaps an occupation. The place of residence is often not accurate and simply records where the accused was captured at the time of the offence. It is usually not the place of origin. Little may be learned about the accused other than the verdict. This may lead to other sources such as gaol deliveries or transportation records. It is usually the case that more is learned about the deponents or witnesses than the person who is on trial.

For all accounts of trials, newspapers are a very good source of information. Scandalous affairs in particular were reported with great relish. An account in a local newspaper may add greatly to the bare bones of the surviving trial record. Such reports can be found in newspapers held in a local library or at British Library Newspapers at Colindale. What is held in the national collection can be discovered through *www.bl.uk/ catalogues/newspapers/datesearch.asp.*

Gaol records

The Criminal Registers (HO 26 and 27 at the National Archives), which mainly date from 1805, list those in prison in the 19th century. Stuart Tamblin is indexing the names for the early part of the century; see *www.fhindexes.co.uk.*

Lists of those held in prisons awaiting trial were often printed, including persons tried by the Quarter Sessions. For those who were then

Smart data: Manorial courts
The court was presided over by the lord of the manor, but if he had many manors to attend to his sheriff (shire reeve) or steward would take charge in his stead. His principal officers, who were responsible for certain areas of the manor, would also attend. For instance, the woodward (wood warden) took care of the woods, just as the hayward was the guardian of the hay and harvest. The catchpole was the forerunner of the policeman, as his job was to apprehend tenants and bring them before the court. Many of these occupations were passed on from father to son and later developed into surnames.

sentenced, the verdict and punishment are recorded. You can look for these in county record offices or in various sources at the National Archives. They are mainly in series PCOM, HO, CRIM and MEPO. Later records may even include a photograph of the prisoner.

Transportation

The National Archives has extensive records of sentences of transportation overseas and, of course, information will be found in the former colony to which they were sent. Records, especially of New South Wales and Tasmania (Van Diemen's Land), should be examined to see what happened to the convict on arrival and after the sentence was completed. The record should contain a physical description, age, perhaps next of kin and place of birth, and the court that passed the sentence, and will enable the trial records to be found and read. Among the records in the National Archives are the convict transportation registers (HO 11) that list those sent to Australia from 1787 to 1867. There are also records of those held on prison hulks awaiting their passage.

Criminal Ancestors: A Guide to Historical Criminal Records in England and Wales by David Hawkings should be read to learn more about the content and use of criminal records in research.

The manorial court

Before the 19th century most of our ancestors lived in rural communities rather than in towns. Whether they were freeholders, leaseholders or held the use of their land directly from the lord of the manor as a copyholder (*see* page 147), they would be subject to the rules and customs set by the customary tenants and their masters. This would govern what they could and could not do in their daily lives.

The proceedings of the various manorial courts will provide snapshots of what a forebear was doing when he or she came into conflict with the lores and laws of the manor. They may also record admission of a tenant to the use of a particular piece of land that could be used for subsistence farming. For a guide to their use in genealogy, read Peter Park's *My Ancestors Were Manorial Tenants: How Can I Find Out More about Them?*

There were two types of manorial court – the Court Leet, which dealt with misdemeanours, and the Court Baron, which dealt with the transfer of the use of manorial land. All manorial tenants were expected to attend the manorial court when it sat. Some tenants were chosen by the community to form the Jurat, or jury. They sat in judgment over the cases brought before them and gave their verdict on their fellow inhabitants. Their names will be listed in the court roll or book for that date.

Other listed names would belong to tenants who were brought before the Court Leet to explain why they had broken the lores of the manor: for instance, by letting their pigs stray on to another person's land, grinding their own corn instead of using the lord's mill, or leaving a ditch unscoured and causing a flood. Although apparently unimportant to our modern way of thinking, these were very significant acts to their fellow tenants. They had to be punished, usually with a monetary fine, and social pressure from the neighbours would make it unlikely that the problem would recur. Most significantly for the family historian, it shows that an ancestor was alive at a given time on that manor.

If the burial of an ancestor is found in the parish register, try looking in the Court Baron section of the appropriate manorial records. The use of his or her copyhold land – so called because the person's right to occupy that land was written in the court records and the person given a copy – would be surrendered back to the lord of the manor for reallocation. The new tenant would be admitted and given a copyhold document. Any relationship to the previous tenant will be stated in the record.

Such records are very useful if the parish registers and/or the bishops' transcripts for that locality have been lost for some reason. There may also be no surviving probate records for that area. Such is the case with Devon, where both bishops' transcripts and wills perished in the bombing in World War II. If the relevant parish has also lost its registers, the manorial court records may provide a unique insight into the lives of the inhabitants.

The Manorial Documents Register, now housed at the National Archives, gives the location of manorial records. First, the names of all manors which lie within the boundary of a given parish must be identified. Once these are known, the listing for each manor shows what records have been identified. Whether these were court rolls or books, maps, lists of tenants or rentals, the Register records the dates of the documents and, most importantly, where they are held. They may be at the National Archives itself, in a county record office or in a private collection. In this way, access can be achieved. The Manorial Documents Register is in the process of being computerized and put online at *www.national archives.gov.uk/mdr.*

The equity courts

Some families spent much of their time arguing with the state or each other. Should yours be a family that delighted in litigation, you have an excellent chance of finding documentation to give you an insight into the cause of their discontent. Not only will it provide a fascinating snapshot of a particular disagreement, it may also provide some genealogical clues.

There were many courts of 'fairness', as the equity courts may be considered. They heard disputes between individuals and the government or Crown, or among groups of people. This argument might have been over land, paying taxes, the content of a will or simply a personal quarrel, and would form the basis of a civil suit today.

Suits were heard by a number of different courts from the 14th to the 19th centuries. Some functioned for only a limited period of time. The most familiar are those of Chancery and Exchequer. Each would have heard a particular type of dispute. Two publications by H. Horwitz, *Chancery Equity Records and Proceedings 1600–1800* and *Exchequer Equity Records and Proceedings 1649–1841*, explain how each court worked.

Although the process of the hearing was very complex, there was a consistent pattern. The court was presided over by a Master in Chancery who decided the outcome. After the declaration of the cause of the dispute, the legal representatives drew up a series of arguments on each side. Once it was decided what evidence needed to be collected, questions or interrogatories were then addressed to the selected witnesses or deponents. These were answered in depositions and eventually, after consideration of the evidence, a judgment or order would be produced. This settled the case. Often, however, despite producing a great deal of work and, no doubt, income for lawyers, no clear conclusion was forthcoming and the case ground to a halt.

The paperwork to be found at the National Archives is unlikely to be stored as a single body of evidence. Not all papers will have survived. For instance, the deponents' answers may exist but not the questions. You need to make a detailed search through the many classes of material to draw together all the strands of a case. Some classes are well indexed or catalogued whilst others are not. In general, if you believe that your family was involved in a Chancery dispute at a given date, this would be a valuable start. Begin with the Order in series C 33 for 1544 to 1875, if it was ever produced. If not, use any available finding aid to the most likely classes for that time period. For further information, read Susan T. Moore, *Family Feuds: An Introduction to Chancery Proceedings*.

Many records are being computerized and put online through the Catalogue or the Equity Pleadings (C 6) sections of the National Archives website at *www.nationalarchives.gov.uk/equity*.

The main finding aid, which allows access to Chancery proceedings and depositions, is the Bernau Index. Compiled in the early 20th century, it includes the published calendars and indexes to many classes of Chancery and Exchequer. It has been filmed by the Mormons and can be searched through one of the family history centres or at the Society of Genealogists. It is a lucky dip, which may lead you to a goldmine of material on a family with a more unusual surname. See *How to Use the Bernau Index* by Hilary Sharpe.

The Exchequer records also contain a huge amount of material on the collection of taxes such as the Hearth Tax, the Subsidies and other collections from the 12th to the 18th centuries. These are mainly in series E 179. This material is the subject of a concerted indexing project which can be viewed on the National Archives website at *www.nationalarchives.gov.uk/e179*.

To punish nonconformists in the 17th century, their lands were confiscated. The proceedings can be found in the Recusant Rolls in E 376 and E 377.

Other courts of equity had specific roles in certain periods. The courts of Star Chamber (records in STAC) and Requests (in series REQ), the poor man's court, sat only from the late 15th century to the beginning of the Civil War in the 1640s.

In 1876, the process of Chancery and Exchequer was taken over by the Supreme Court of Justice and the records are in class J. Decrees and Orders for 1876 to 1955 are in series J 15. Long-running disputes which were still the subject of litigation when the change occurred may have had all their records transferred to the new authority. Such records may include very detailed evidence such as birth, marriage or death certificates as well as wills.

The parish

The parish officials were responsible for the maintenance of each parish church and chapel and the spiritual and moral lives of the parishioners. Funds were collected through rates, tithes, fines and charitable bequests to pay for the structure of the church and to remunerate those who worked for the parish. The money was also used to relieve those who were entitled to be living there during any hard times that they might have experienced.

Before 1834, those who were likely to become recipients of parish funding through the Poor Law would be examined. Enquiry was made into their legal place of settlement. This right of abode was claimed through place of birth, apprenticeship, working or renting property in the parish, serving as a parish official or the marriage of a woman to a parishioner who was legally entitled to be there. The wandering poor, who could not prove their right to be in a parish, could be removed to another parish where they had a claim to settlement. The hearing would have resulted in the production of very valuable Poor Law documents, such as settlement examinations and removal orders. These documented the movement of the lower classes about the country. They recorded place of birth and age for the examinant, and the names, ages and places of birth of his dependent wife and children.

Those who were intending to move from one parish to another may have taken with them a settlement certificate. This ensured that the home parish, which had already accepted them as its legal inhabitants, would be prepared to take them back and look after them should they fall upon hard times. This was not a document for paupers but rather for those seeking a new home and opportunities away from their previous parish of abode. Once again, if it has survived, it will provide very valuable clues to where someone was born or where they had gained a place of settlement.

In the case of an illegitimate child, the Overseers of the Poor would seek to reduce a possible long-term burden on their funds by trying to remove mother and baby back to the mother's place of settlement. If she was legally entitled to be in the parish, the Overseers would seek another source of upkeep by tracing the supposed father. Their enquiries would have resulted in bastardy examinations and orders and, in the case of the fathers who did not do their duty, warrants for apprehension. This can often suggest the most likely or accepted father of an illegitimate child (*see* Chapter 1). Such children may then have been apprenticed to a local tradesman or landowner (*see* Chapter 2).

Other officials, such as constables, were employed to enforce the Overseers' decisions. From the paperwork generated, such as the vestry, churchwardens', Overseers' and constables' accounts and minutes, you may be able to discover how your ancestors contributed to the life of the church itself, or the parish in general. They might have paid towards the upkeep of the fabric of the parish or provided a particular service to the community, such as killing vermin or washing vestments. It is not unusual to see them 'grassing' or informing on fellow parishioners. The records also detail disbursements to the needy poor.

Every time that a person is recorded doing something at a certain place on a certain date, this provides a form of census, giving evidence of who is living where at a particular time.

Poor Law records will be found in the appropriate county record office, if they have survived, and will have been catalogued along with the more frequently consulted parish registers. The Church of Jesus Christ of Latter-day Saints has filmed some of these documents. Subsequently, the decisions of the parish hierarchy were notified to the Quarter Sessions or, if it involved the morals of the parishioners, to the ecclesiastical court. Those authorities may have pursued the matter further.

From 1834, the New Poor Law established Poor Law Unions with Boards of Guardians. These were groupings of parishes that were to enforce the new laws. Workhouses were built to provide for the poor. Admission and discharge registers and other records are to be found in county record offices and provide genealogical information about those who were taken in or who died there. Children were often born in the workhouse, too.

Other records are to be found at the National Archives. The records of the Poor Law Unions include information about the staff of the workhouse and the paupers. The most valuable genealogical material is in class MH 12, which is Poor Law Union Correspondence dating from 1834 to about 1900. Inmates were sometimes encouraged to find a new life abroad and the state paid for them to emigrate. This was a cheaper alternative to keeping them at home.

Surviving records for each union are listed in *Poor Law Unions* (4 volumes) by Jeremy Gibson, Colin Rogers and Cliff Webb.

The ecclesiastical court

The church courts are familiar to family historians as they dealt with the process of probate by proving wills and granting letters of administration (*see* Chapter 7), issuing marriage bonds, allegations and licences and, in some cases, divorces or annulments (*see* Chapter 3). However, these courts also had jurisdiction over many other aspects of the moral lives of our forebears. They issued licences to those who looked after the religious well-being of the people. These were preachers, teachers and midwives. The last group was responsible for baptizing sick children who died before being properly accepted into the Church of England. Colin Chapman's *Sin, Sex and Probate: Ecclesiastical Courts, Their Officials and Their Records* describes their functions in depth.

The incidents heard or the cases of misconduct processed by the ecclesiastical courts involved those who had not done their duty or had broken the church laws. Thus, vicars could be brought before the court to answer for the irregularity of the marriage ceremonies that they had conducted, perhaps without banns or licence.

Parishioners were prosecuted for committing fornication or adultery and for producing illegitimate children. There were disputes over non-payment of tithes, especially by nonconformists. Deponents were called to give evidence to assist the court to come to its conclusion. If your ancestor was a witness, he would have provided a statement of his age, place of birth and length of residence in the parish. This may provide invaluable genealogical evidence. Since you cannot know who appeared at a particular enquiry, you should consult any index that has been produced to the deponents.

These fascinating court records will usually be found in the diocesan record office. This will be wherever the bishops' or archdeacons' transcripts, marriage licences, bonds or allegations and probate material are kept for that ecclesiastical authority.

Smart reading on court records

Chancery Equity Records and Proceedings 1600–1800, by H. Horwitz, 2nd edn (Public Record Office, 1998)

Criminal Ancestors: A Guide to Historical Criminal Records in England and Wales, by David Hawkings (Sutton, 1996)

Exchequer Equity Records and Proceedings 1649–1841, by H. Horwitz (Public Record Office, 2001)

Family Feuds: An Introduction to Chancery Proceedings, by Susan T. Moore (Federation of Family History Societies, 2003)

How to Use the Bernau Index, by Hilary Sharpe (Society of Genealogists, 1996)

My Ancestors Were Manorial Tenants: How Can I Find Out More about Them?, by Peter Park (Society of Genealogists, 2001)

Poor Law Unions, by Jeremy Gibson, Colin Rogers and Cliff Webb, 2nd edn (Federation of Family History Societies, 1993–2000), 4 vols

Quarter Sessions Records for Family Historians: A Select List, by Jeremy Gibson, 2nd edn (Federation of Family History Societies, 2000)

Sin, Sex and Probate: Ecclesiastical Courts, Their Officials and Their Records, by Colin Chapman, 2nd edn (Lochin, 1997)

Specialist Indexes for Family Historians, by Jeremy Gibson, 2nd edn (Federation of Family History Societies, 2000)

Chapter 6

A matter of status

- Directories
- Poll books and electoral rolls
- Taxes
- Hearth Tax
- Land Tax
- Sequestration and compounding
- Oaths
- Naturalization
- Freemen
- Boyd's Inhabitants of London
- Other collections at the Society of Genealogists
- Heraldic visitations and records
- Occupational sources
- Record sources for professions
- Trades and occupations

Once an ancestor has embarked on a career and established himself in life, he is likely to be easier to find. Any reference to the trade, profession or status of an ancestor in his community will enable new information to be discovered about his life or genealogy. You should take all steps to document the working life of an ancestor and his position in society – you never know what this might reveal until you look.

Directories

One of the first sources to use to look for an ancestor is the commercial directory. These directories date from the late 17th century for London and listings of the principal inhabitants and tradesmen were produced for all cities and market towns by the mid to late 18th century. By the mid-19th century, a number of different companies, such as Kelly, White and Pigot, were producing regular publications for cities or counties.

A city directory is generally divided into separate sections. The court section lists those who were members of the nobility or the gentry and those who were of independent means, being members of the more notable professions, such as doctors or clerics. For tradesmen there is a general alphabetical or commercial index. This will have been rearranged into sections for different trades. A fourth section lists those who have submitted their names and details by the address at which they lived or traded. There is also a description of the main establishments in the city, such as schools, churches and other civic amenities, with their date of establishment.

A county directory provides a detailed description of each parish, stating, for instance, the dedication of the churches there and the dates of their surviving parish registers. Nonconformist chapels and schools are listed. You can learn other important information, such as the Poor Law Union and ecclesiastical jurisdiction in which it was situated. Reference will have been made to any important trades that were commonly practised there. There are then two separate lists of the main inhabitants. The first records the nobility, gentry and important residents, whilst the second lists the farmers and tradesmen. In larger parishes, these may be subdivided by occupation. Most inhabitants, who were employed by the tradesmen, are not listed in directories.

Such directories can be used to track the career, address, movement and change in status of our ancestors. A sudden disappearance from a directory of a city or county may suggest a migration to another county, perhaps to another place where that trade or occupation was commonly practised, or that the person had died. The addresses can be a valuable way of finding the person in a Victorian census, especially in a large city or town for which there is no surname index or when his name has been misindexed in a national census index (*see* Chapter 3). Many directories have now been made available on CD-ROM or microfiche. These are available for research in record offices and libraries.

The University of Leicester, at *www.historical directories.org*, runs a project to make images of commercial directories available online from 1750 to 1919. Each directory is searchable by surname.

For the period before commercial directories were produced nationally, you should make use of any guide to the history of the county. This might have been written by a local antiquarian and will provide invaluable information about the parish where your ancestors lived. A helpful source is *The Victoria History of the Counties of England* for that particular county, if it has been published. Useful information is recorded about each parish, describing the church and its monuments, charities, manors and their lords and other local history. You will find documented genealogical information about the principal families that lived in the parish. Of course, in general it is only the landed classes who were included.

Poll books and electoral rolls

One entitlement of those who had been successful in life was to determine who should represent them in government or on a local authority. The right to vote at an election was bestowed by a property qualification, by being a freeman of a company, guild or city or, later, by age. The electorate of the earlier centuries was usually limited to males of full age who owned land. Later this was extended to those who had achieved a level of status in the community and who were paying rates. This varied, depending on the type of election and, of course, the date. It was not until 1918 that all men of 21 and over and women aged 30 and upward who owned property, or were the wives of householders, were entitled to vote in national elections, irrespective of status. Universal franchise for women over 21 was granted in 1928.

How someone voted was recorded in poll books from the early 18th century (generally 1711) to the introduction of the secret ballot in 1872. Poll books can be found in many different local and national libraries as well as county record offices. Their location is noted by Jeremy Gibson and Colin Rogers in *Poll Books c.1696–1872: A Directory to Holdings in Great Britain*. These can be valuable in providing an address for an ancestor and discovering his political leaning.

From 1832, electoral rolls were required to be compiled and published. These recorded the name of the registered elector, his or her address and by what method they were qualified to vote. Electoral rolls can be consulted in libraries and county record offices or at the British Library. Gibson and Rogers outline where they can be found in *Electoral Registers since 1832 and Burgess Rolls*. Again, these can be used in conjunction with the censuses of the 19th century. From 1832 to 1872, you can look for your ancestor in both electoral rolls and poll books.

A modern listing of those found in electoral rolls and telephone directories can be found on the annual editions of *UK-Info disk* on CD-ROM. The disks for the last few years can be used on the first floor at the Family Records Centre. They are particularly useful for tracing modern addresses for relatives who may have family documents and memorabilia.

Taxes

The financial burden of having made progress in life was to pay taxes and rates. Before 1834, at the parish level, an inhabitant who was not a pauper was required to pay the poor rate. The names and contribution of those who paid would be recorded in the parish accounts (*see* Chapter 5).

On a regional or national level, other taxes were collected at different times. Many different taxes have been levied throughout the centuries, some being collected more peacefully and more comprehensively than others. These include the Lay Subsidies of the 12th to 17th centuries and the Poll Taxes of the 14th, 17th and early 18th centuries. Various taxes were imposed on our 17th-century ancestors to pay for the troubles occasioned by the Civil War. There were many special levies, including taxes on male servants (1777–1852), hair powder (1795–1861) and windows (1696–1851). Records of these taxes can reveal that an ancestor flourished in a given place at a certain time, despite having to pay some of his hard-earned cash to the state. Many only have local or partial survival. Some are to be found in the local county record office, whilst others are in the National Archives, mainly in the Exchequer or

Treasury classes, particularly E 179 or T 47. They may have been indexed locally and even published. If so, these will provide a method of locating the person you seek relatively easily. Those in class E 179 can be located through the National Archives database *www.national archives.gov.uk/e179*, dedicated to that class of records.

Other taxation records are much more useful to the genealogist and family historian because their survival and coverage of the population is more widespread.

Hearth Tax

From 1662 to 1689, a tax on fireplaces was levied. Lists were maintained by the parish constable and submitted twice yearly to the Quarter Sessions and then to the Exchequer. Thus, records of both those who paid the tax and those who were exempt on the grounds of their poverty can be found in both the county record office and the National Archives (series E 179) respectively. These can be used to show that a person was alive in a given parish at a certain point in the second half of the 17th century, just after the restoration of the monarchy and the enormous disturbance caused by the Civil War.

The number of hearths on which a householder was taxed provides an idea of his social standing or status within the community. Many surviving lists have been transcribed, indexed and published. A guide to their content and use in family history can be found in Jeremy Gibson's *Hearth Tax Returns, Other Later Stuart Tax Lists and the Association Oath Rolls*.

Land Tax

Levied from 1693 to 1963, this tax covered three centuries of the lives of our ancestors. The most extensive records exist for 1780 to 1832. This was an important period for this form of taxation since those who paid it had reached a certain standing in the community, based on the value of their real estate. This entitled them to vote (*see* page 165). These lists survive in the Quarter Sessions records, and from 1772 show not only the owner but also the person who occupied the property. The records can be located by using *Land and Window Tax Assessments* by Jeremy Gibson, Mervyn Medlycott and Dennis Mills.

From 1832, when the publication of electoral rolls was formalized, the return of the Land Tax assessments to the Sessions was no longer essential for maintaining the list of those entitled to the franchise. Many were still returned, however. From 1798, future Land Tax payments could be commuted to a one-off payment, payable in instalments if required. These records exist in the National Archives IR 22 to IR 24 and list the landowner and occupier in that one year alone, sometimes with a map of the property. After 1832, those who had taken this option do not appear in the Land Tax returns.

Other local taxes might have been levied for the maintenance of the fabric and services to the street where a property was situated. These could have maintained sewers, paving or lighting. Once more, records will show the address, the owner and occupier of the particular dwelling and can be found in the appropriate county record office.

Sequestration and compounding

During the English Civil War in the 17th century – a particularly difficult period for genealogical research due to the loss of many of the usual types of record – a body of records exists for those whose lands and property were confiscated because of their allegiance to the Crown. The estates of Royalists, as well as those of the

Crown and the Church, were seized by the Parliamentary authorities through the Sequestration and Compounding Committees. Commonly known as Royalist Composition Papers, the records, which detail the estates and families of those under investigation, are in class SP 23 at the National Archives. *Calendars of the Proceedings of the Committee for Compounding 1643–1660* were published in five volumes. The name index in volume 5 is available on microfiche from the Society of Genealogists.

Oaths

People were required to swear a number of oaths that reflected their allegiance to the Crown in the 17th century. The most useful of these records are the Protestation Returns collected in early 1642. They supposedly listed all men over 18 who swore the oaths, but often also included those who refused to swear. Such men might have been nonconformists who could not swear that they believed in the authority of the Church of England. For this reason, they may not appear in the parish registers of the time. Where the Returns survive for the area where your ancestor lived, they may provide proof that he was alive at the beginning of the Civil War. The original records are in the House of Lords Record Office. Many have been indexed and published. A guide to these records and those of the other oaths of this period is in *The Protestation Returns 1641–42 and Other Contemporary Listings* by Jeremy Gibson and Alan Dell.

Naturalization

If your ancestor came into this country as a permanent immigrant, he or she may have chosen to become a British subject through naturalization. Most immigrants did not become naturalized. If someone is stated in a census to have been a 'British Subject', this may be a clue to the completion of that process. Although only the country of birth was recorded in a Victorian enumeration, the naturalization certificate and documents often record the exact date and place of birth and parentage, together with other genealogical information about relatives. These are mainly in the National Archives from 1844 to 1948 in various HO series. Those after 1922 are closed to public inspection. Before 1844, those taking oaths of allegiance are recorded in C 65–67 and other classes (*see* the National Archives Domestic Records Information Leaflet 49 *Naturalisation and Citizenship: Grants of British*

Nationality). Their names were printed in the *London Gazette*.

There are printed indexes for 1509 to 1800 in the Huguenot Society of Great Britain and Ireland publications, volumes 8, 18 and 27. For years from 1801 to 1936, there are indexes available on the first floor at the Family Records Centre. This is extended to 1980 at the National Archives.

The certificates and papers from 1844 to 1930 can be searched by name through *www.national archives.gov.uk/catalogue*.

For those who came here from the Caribbean, South Asia or Ireland or who were Jewish, a useful internet source is *www.movinghere. org.uk*.

Freemen

Valued members of society were those who had become important in their trade, town or city. Besides being economically important to the livelihood and economic prosperity of the community, they would also pass on their knowledge and experience to the next and future generations. This was through taking on apprentices of their own or by endowing the foundation of guild or charity schools. The freeman had the right to elect the officers of that organization. In

Smart data: Freemen

Men who lived in larger towns and the cities aspired to become a freeman of a trade guild and of the city or borough. Freedomship could be achieved in the following ways: servitude (completing an apprenticeship to a freeman – see Chapter 2), patrimony (where the right was through birth as the child of a current freeman), redemption (purchasing the admission to freedom) and, in some places, marriage to the daughter of another freeman. Often a freeman of a company would have progressed to become a freeman of the city. Once he had achieved that status, the freeman could take on apprentices of his own and vote in municipal elections. The records of freemen can be used to distinguish between those with the same name who lived in a civic area at the same time.

addition, through his right to vote in elections, he could elect the officials who governed the borough or city and even the country (see Poll Books and Electoral Rolls on page 165).

The names of the freemen are recorded in the rolls or admission lists, together with the date and method of entry. The trade of the member, perhaps his age, and sometimes parentage or at least the name of his father if entry was by patrimony or even apprenticeship, can be stated. These will be found in the local county record office that holds the records of that city or town. Many have been transcribed, indexed and published.

Those records for freemen of trades or professions of the City of London are at Guildhall Library. A guide to these records is *My Ancestors Were Freemen of the City of London* by V.E. Aldous. The records are catalogued online at *www.history.ac.uk/gh/livlist.htm* and this site includes printed accounts and lists of the membership of each company. Those who became freemen of the City of London itself can be accessed through the 14 index volumes that cover the period of 1681 to 1940. The names are arranged by the first letter of the freeman's surname and record the month of admission, method of entry and, most importantly, the company to which the freeman belonged. The associated admission papers for the applicant include genealogical information such as age and place of birth as well as his father's name. These records are now at the London Metropolitan Archives, having been transferred there from the Corporation of London Records Office. By learning the name of his company, you can search other records in Guildhall Library.

The freemen would pay subscriptions or quarterage to the company. Those records show that they were still active in the company. Failure to pay could suggest retirement from business, or death. This can lead to a search for a death, burial or probate document (*see* Chapter 7).

Boyd's Inhabitants of London

Also known as Citizens of London, this enormous work of Percival Boyd consists of 238 volumes of information compiled about those who lived and thrived in London from the 15th to the 19th centuries. Many were freemen of London companies. It contains 60,000 indexed birth briefs (printed forms) recording information about the person collected from guild records, parish registers, marriage licences and probate records. Where known, it also documents their children. You may be pointed to other printed material on the family such as that to be found in heraldic visitations (*see* oposite) and county genealogies. This invaluable source can be used at the Society of Genealogists. As that library holds many books from Boyd's own genealogical collection, his cross-referenced annotations to the relevant page in Boyd's Inhabitants can allow access from another direction.

Other collections at the Society of Genealogists

Within the Society, there are many other very useful collections which may include material on all sorts of families, usually high up on the social scale. These should be examined to see if new clues can be found. There are large and small pedigree rolls. The Documents Collection includes collections of research notes, copies of certificates and wills and listings made from all sorts of original sources. There are Special Collections, representing the lifetime's work of a professional genealogist or of someone who has dedicated their time to learning as much as possible about those with a particular surname. There are also many individual small Family History Tracts and an extensive collection of rather larger published Family Histories in which your ancestors may be found. Do not neglect these.

Heraldic visitations and records

Many who were of sufficient status to play a very important role in the life of a parish, town or city were either titled or members of the aristocracy. They may have used a coat-of-arms. The records of such armigerous people can be very valuable in unearthing genealogical material about those ancestors who made such claims. Beware that many of the nouveau riche of the 18th and 19th centuries, having been very successful, assumed arms without having any right to use them through a grant at the College of Arms. Where proper application was made and arms were granted, this was recorded there. You may be able to find other associated genealogical material about the original grantee, his relatives and descendants by commissioning a search in the collections in its library at *www.college-of-arms.gov.uk*. A pedigree of the family may have been placed on record there.

From 1530 to 1688, the heralds undertook periodic visitations to each of the counties, about every 20 or 30 years. They recorded those who were considered to be using arms correctly and may also have listed those who were refused the coat-of-arms because they could not prove their right to them, usually through descent. At the same time, a pedigree of the family was recorded. This may have been oral or may have been backed up by reference to family papers. The original material or later copies may survive in the College of Arms, the British Library and other major archives and libraries.

C.R. Humphery-Smith's *Armigerous ancestors* provides a listing of where the original material may be found. It also includes a reprint of R. Sims' *Index to the Pedigrees Contained in the Heralds' Visitations and Other Manuscripts in the British Museum* (1849) which can be valuable in locating original pedigrees.

The Harleian Society has printed many visitation pedigrees. Others are included in county histories and county genealogies, or are to be found published by county record societies or in the serial periodicals of the 19th century. To access these, the researcher should make use of the Genealogists' Guides to printed genealogical and heraldic material (*see* the reading list at the end of the chapter).

These may also lead the researcher to other pedigrees and accounts of the history of the family and its branches to be found in the various publications of Burke, Debrett, Walford, etc. This includes those where the title may have become extinct or dormant.

Many pedigrees have been annotated with references to other documentation. These may include monumental inscriptions or even inquisitions post mortem. These inquisitions were held from the 13th to the 17th centuries to establish the property and rightful heirs of tenants-in-chief to the Crown. They are held at the National Archives in C 132–142 and E 149–150. There are also separate records for the Palatinates of Chester and Durham and the Duchy of Lancaster. The earlier calendars and some records for specific counties are published.

Occupational sources

Whatever the trade, profession or occupation that our ancestors pursued in their lifetimes, there are a range of sources or indexes available, in either original or printed form, in public or private hands, which should be accessed or consulted to find out about their careers. The records may add to our knowledge of their genealogy and relatives.

A statement made at his or her marriage, death or burial, or recorded at the baptism or birth, marriage, death or burial of a child, should identify the career that your ancestor practised. A trade or profession can be located in census returns, at enlistment into a service or in a will.

Stuart Raymond has collected together titles of printed accounts of occupational sources. These are found in his publication *Occupational Sources for Genealogists*. A useful guide to those who lived in the capital city is *Londoners' Occupations: A Genealogical Guide*. For other areas of England and Wales, consult the occupational section in Raymond's specific guides to each county in the *British Genealogical Bibliographies* series, where they have been produced.

Many unique indexes are being compiled to those involved in particular trades or occupations. There are indexes for coastguards, brickmakers, entertainers and many more. These can be identified and a search requested through *Specialist Indexes for Family Historians* by Jeremy Gibson and Elizabeth Hampson.

Record sources for professions

Many professions have specific regulatory bodies which historically governed and qualified practitioners. For doctors, surgeons, nurses and other medics such as apothecaries, vets and pharmacists; for lawyers and barristers; and for teachers, bodies were established to examine and ensure the good practice of the profession's members.

Each organization kept records. It is worth consulting the governing body to see what records are in existence for a person who followed a profession. Some of these bodies published annual lists of their members, such as *The Law List*, *The Medical Directory* or *The Medical Register*, *Dentists' Register*, etc.

Other publications are cumulative lists of those who were practitioners over a given time period or at a particular date. Thus, we have, for barristers, Joseph Foster's *Men at the Bar* compiled in 1885 or *The Roll of the Royal College of Physicians of London* by W. Munk published in 1878, which includes biographical sketches of physicians from 1518 to 1825.

Some professions have produced listings of those who were mentioned in their documentary material. Thus, practitioners may have obtained a licence or taken out a subscription to a publication at some point in their working careers. For instance, those loosely involved in the treatment of the sick, such as spectacle-makers, apothecaries and midwives, as well as doctors and surgeons, are included in Wallis and Wallis's *Eighteenth Century Medics*.

For other groups, such as nurses (1921–73), barber-surgeons (1540–1745) and teachers (1902–48), there are listings of those who were qualified by these bodies, but these have not been published. The original records need to be examined wherever they are now stored. In the cases of the above professions, they are at the National Archives, Guildhall Library and Society of Genealogists respectively. The last of these libraries also holds a wealth of material for those applying for a career in the Civil Service. The so-called 'Evidences of Age' includes details of some 70,000 men from 1855 to the 1930s required to produce information about their addresses and certified evidence of their baptism or birth.

Those who became clerics, nonconformist ministers and Catholic priests and nuns have left records. *The Clergy List* and *Crockford's Clerical Directory* are well-known sources for bishops, vicars and curates. Clerics were licensed, promoted and posted to new livings by the ecclesiastical authorities. These records can be tracked down. For a short period, Joseph Foster accumulated and published these in his *Index Ecclesiasticus* for the period of 1800–40.

Many professionals attended one of the principal schools, universities or colleges before settling on their final career. Details of their training, degree, parentage, spouses and subsequent life as a lawyer, doctor, cleric or civil servant will be summarized in any printed alumni of the relevant academic body (*see* Chapter 2).

Trades and occupations

Accounts of the lives of many men and women eminent in their chosen field are to be found in *The Oxford Dictionary of National Biography.* Others may be found in a work on the principal practitioners of a specific craft or profession such as *Who's Who in ...* or *Who Was Who in ...* For some fields, there are acknowledged biographical works such as Grove's *Dictionary of Music and Musicians* or Baillie's *Watchmakers and Clock-makers of the World*.

For other trades or professions, the researcher needs to visit the archive or museum dedicated to keeping its records, such as those for postmen and theatre entertainers. Records of those who were employed as metropolitan policemen, as excise men or on the railways can be found and searched at the National Archives. Some trades and professions will have very good records for all. For others, the material available will depend on the part of the workforce in which the person was employed or the period in which they served.

Look for a book that tells you how to set about tracing the history of your ancestor who followed a given trade or profession. This could be a glossy volume that includes photographs or reproductions of records and documents, or a pamphlet that guides you to the major archives, their content and how to track the life of someone who was engaged in a particular occupation. Whatever the format, it should be read for new ideas.

Also look for a specialist collection of material relating to a particular vocation or occupation and those who practised it. Many libraries hold unique collections that can shed new light on people who were involved in a skill or craft. To discover where such documentation can be found or to contact a person who may have the answer you seek, use *The Aslib Directory of Information Sources in the UK* by Keith Reynard. This lists the libraries, collections and journals of institutes, organizations and associations.

A search on the internet may also lead you to a new source, individual or organization that can help in your research. Does the organization or company which employed your ancestor still exist? If so, where are its records? The National Register of Archives at the National Archives can be used to find the present location of the records of a company by using *www.national archives.gov.uk/nra.* The Business Archives Council, *www.businessarchivescouncil.com*, can also be a way of tracking down surviving records of larger companies. Further ideas for finding this type of record are expounded in *Company and Business Records for Family Historians* by Eric Probert.

Smart reading on work and tax records

Armigerous Ancestors, by C.R. Humphery-Smith (Institute of Heraldic and Genealogical Studies, 1997)

The Aslib Directory of Information Sources in the UK, by Keith Reynard, 13th edn (Europa Publications, 2004)

British Genealogical Bibliographies series, by Stuart Raymond (Federation of Family History Societies)

Calendars of the Proceedings of the Committee for Compounding 1643–1660 (HMSO, 1889–92)

Company and Business Records for Family Historians, by Eric Probert (Federation of Family History Societies, 1994)

Eighteenth Century Medics, by P.J. Wallis and R.V. Wallis, 2nd edn (Project for Historical Biobibliography, 1988)

Electoral Registers since 1832 and Burgess Rolls, by Jeremy Gibson and Colin Rogers, 2nd edn (Federation of Family History Societies, 1990)

A Genealogical Guide: An Index to British Pedigrees in Continuation of Marshall's Genealogists' Guide, by J.B. Whitmore (Walford Brothers, 1953)

The Genealogists' Guide, by G.W. Marshall, 4th edn (reprint, Genealogical Publishing, 1903)

The Genealogist's Guide: An Index to Printed British Pedigrees and Family Histories 1950–75, by G.B. Barrow (Research Publishing, 1977)

Hearth Tax Returns, Other Later Stuart Tax Lists and the Association Oath Rolls, by Jeremy Gibson, 2nd edn (Federation of Family History Societies, 1996)

Index Ecclesiasticus, by Joseph Foster (Parker, 1840)

Land and Window Tax Assessments, by Jeremy Gibson, Mervyn Medlycott and Dennis Mills, 2nd edn (Federation of Family History Societies, 1998)

Londoners' Occupations: A Genealogical Guide, by Stuart Raymond, 2nd edn (Federation of Family History Societies, 2001)

Men at the Bar, by Joseph Foster (Reeves and Turner, 1885)

My Ancestors Were Freemen of the City of London, by V.E. Aldous (Society of Genealogists, 1999)

Naturalisation and Citizenship: Grants of British Nationality, Domestic Records Information Leaflet 49 (The National Archives, 2002)

The New Grove Dictionary of Music and Musicians, edited by Stanley Sadie and John Tyrrell, 2nd edn (Oxford University Press, 2001), 29 vols

Occupational Sources for Genealogists, by Stuart Raymond, 3rd edn (Federation of Family History Societies, 1997)

The Oxford Dictionary of National Biography (Oxford University Press, 2004; also available online by subscription)

Poll Books c.1696–1872: A Directory to Holdings in Great Britain, by Jeremy Gibson and Colin Rogers, 3rd edn (Federation of Family History Societies, 1994)

The Protestation Returns 1641–42 and Other Contemporary Listings, by Jeremy Gibson and Alan Dell (Federation of Family History Societies, 1995)

The Roll of the Royal College of Physicians of London, by W. Munk (Royal College of Physicians, 1878)

Specialist Indexes for Family Historians, by Jeremy Gibson and Elizabeth Hampson, 2nd edn (Federation of Family History Societies, 2000)

Watchmakers and Clockmakers of the World, G.H. Baillie and Brian Loomes (NAG Press, 1988), 2 vols.

Chapter 7

Passing away

- The death certificate
- Deaths outside England and Wales
- Burials
- Nonconformist burials
- Monumental inscriptions
- Obituaries
- Probate records
- Wills after 1858
- Wills before 1858
- Inland Revenue and Estate Duty

When people die, they are buried or cremated, and usually leave some form of probate document. Some may be commemorated on a monumental inscription or by an obituary in a newspaper. Any of these sources will provide valuable clues to their history.

The death certificate

Why would we want to look for a death certificate for any of our ancestors who died after civil registration began on 1 July 1837? Because, until it has been shown that a person died at a particular place on a given day, it cannot be proved that an individual, whose birth or baptism has been found, lived long enough to become an ancestor. Most family trees have on them forebears who apparently never died. Until each has been safely laid to rest, it cannot be shown for certain that they lived beyond infancy and reached child-bearing age. It would be hoped that for every birth or baptism, an equivalent death or burial can be identified.

Unfortunately, in England and Wales, death registration until the June quarter of 1969 required only sparse information to be recorded about the deceased. As only the date, age and cause of death were recorded for all, it can be a disappointing end to a painstaking search through so many years in the quarterly indexes. Since the indexes only record the district, volume number and page on which the entry can be found, it may be very difficult, if not almost impossible, to find and obtain the death certificate of an ancestor who bore a very common name. This is especially true before 1866 when even the age of the person is not given in the indexes. From the September quarter of 1910 to the March quarter of 1969, only the first forename along with the surname is included in full. This makes our search even more difficult. Many people give up and leave the death of the person unresolved.

Does it matter? Yes! The information recorded can provide an address where the person lived near the end their life. If the family can be found at that address in a decennial census, we may determine valuable information about the relatives they lived with. Their places of birth may enable new information to be found. In the case of infants, the father or mother's name may be recorded. For married people, their marital status may, at least, narrow down the period in which their spouse died or even provide evidence of a previously unknown other spouse whom the person had married late in their life. The age or cause of death may be important if the family has a genetic abnormality or susceptibility to a disease. This could be the subject of your study.

If the person died in a hospital, survival, location and access to the records can be determined through *www.nationalarchives.gov.uk/hospital records*, but these could be closed or may have been destroyed. A death in an institution, such as the workhouse or an asylum, may enable other records to be found, probably in the county record office (*see* Chapter 5). If the death was mysterious in any way, a coroner's inquest would have been held. Those records may not have survived or may remain closed to inspection. Their availability and location can be established by reference to *Coroners' Records in England and Wales* by Jeremy Gibson and Colin Rogers. If the coroner's records have not survived, look for a report in the local newspaper. Reports published on the coroner's hearing are often more informative than the official records. It is easy to find accounts in local papers if the exact date and place are known, and in the case of inquests this information is recorded on the death certificate.

From the June quarter of 1969, the informant was required to record where and when the deceased was born. In the case of married women, their maiden surname is included. The date of birth is shown in the national indexes. The extra information, if accurately known and registered, becomes extremely valuable if a search in the birth indexes for England and Wales has been unsuccessful. The new information may suggest a new place of birth, a different age or even a new surname to try. In many cases, the researcher may now know that the person was not born in England or Wales, but in Scotland, Ireland or abroad.

The usual shortcuts and indexes to locate entries in the indexes of General Registration previously discussed in the case of births (*see* Chapter 1) and marriages (*see* Chapter 3) are equally applicable to the search for deaths.

It is always worth trying *http://freebmd. rootsweb.com* for those who probably died in the period of 1837 to about 1910. You can search a long period very easily. Use wildcard searches in case the name was misindexed or is under a spelling variant. If the name was very common, you can search in a limited geographic area.

You can pay for *www.familyrelatives.org* to search for death references that should have occurred in a certain period. This stops you from having to search arduously, quarter by quarter, through each index volume. The search will be done for you and the results presented to you.

Smart data: Indexes to overseas deaths

Army deaths	1796–1965
Boer War deaths	1899–1902
WWI deaths	1914–21 (Army officers; Army other ranks; Royal Navy, all ranks; Indian Services)
WWII deaths	1939–48 (Army officers; Army other ranks; Royal Navy officers; Royal Navy ratings; RAF; Indian Services)
Marine deaths	1837–1965
Consular deaths	1849–1965
UK High Commission	1950–65
Air deaths	1947–65
Deaths abroad (includes all the types of record listed above)	1966 onwards

If the entry is not found in either of these partial indexes, and if you do not have access in book form at the Family Records Centre or through a microfiche (or even a microfilm) copy of the indexes at a local library or record office, use the pay-for-view indexes. Both *www.bmdindex.*

co.uk and *www.1837online.com* allow you to view the complete copy of the indexes from 1837 to the present, page by page. If the name of the deceased is too common and the probable place of death is known, you may be able to search indexes to the required county or registration district through *www.ukbmd.org.uk.*

You can obtain copies of certified entries for any suitable reference through those sites, which provide an online ordering service. Alternatively, the GRO's own site *www.gro.gov.uk* can be used.

Deaths outside England and Wales

The Miscellaneous Section of the records at the Family Records Centre should not be neglected. Many of our male ancestors died in, or as the result of, the many conflicts that the British have fought over the past two centuries. Others were working abroad when they met their end. The indexes to the Miscellaneous Section are included on the 1837Online site at *www.1837 online.com.*

For those soldiers, sailors, airmen and, indeed, civilians who died as a result of enemy action and who are commemorated on a monument or war memorial, the website of the Commonwealth War Graves Commission, *www.*

cwgc.org, can provide parentage and civilian addresses or allow you to identify your serviceman among the many men (and some women) with the same name who are listed in the very sparse indexes to war deaths. For the many men who died in the World War I, it is also worth examining *Soldiers Died in the Great War* (Naval and Military Press) on compact disk.

If, after extensive searches have been made through the records of England and Wales, no results have been found, the possibility must be considered that the person died elsewhere. They may have died in Scotland, where records begin in 1855; Ireland from 1864; Northern Ireland 1922; the Isle of Man 1849; the Channel Islands from as early as 1840. The details registered at a death in Scotland, especially in the first year of 1855, are much fuller than those south of the border.

The person you are seeking may have died in another country. Many British who died abroad will be found in the records of the Indian sub-continent at the India Office Records in the Asia, Pacific and Africa Collections at the British Library. These are actually burial records, but often include the date of death.

The Non-Statutory Returns also include deaths of some of those Britons who died abroad. Dating from as early as 1707, they are to be found in RG 32–36, and indexed in RG 43/3–6 and 10–14 at the Family Records Centre and the National Archives. Some war deaths are included in RG 32 and RG 35.

The International Memoranda at Guildhall Library, covering the period from 1816 to 1924, include some burials of those who died abroad and who were notified to British chaplains and embassies. These are contained and indexed in MS 10926, 11224 and 23607.

Besides those events notified to the English authorities, many other Britons died abroad but do not appear in these sources. Their deaths may be located through the records of general or local registration in the appropriate county, state, province or town. The *International Vital Records Handbook* by Thomas Jay Kemp can be very useful in learning the dates of such records and contacting the relevant authority.

It must be stressed that the content of death records and certificates produced by other countries or areas may be much more informative genealogically than those available here. If a branch of the family left for Australia, for instance, it is imperative that their death certificates are obtained. These may record the names of both parents of someone who died at a very old age, the date and place of his or her marriage and the names and ages of all of his or her offspring, both alive and dead. If this person shared the same parentage as one who remained in this country, extremely valuable information will be located which will dramatically aid future investigations.

Burials

For those who died before the introduction of civil registration or, indeed, for those who died after July 1837, their burial record should be sought. This is clearly much easier to do if the family lived in a rural, sparsely populated parish than if they died in somewhere like St Pancras or Spitalfields in London. By the mid-19th century, many thousands were laid to rest each year. Where were they all buried, since the available space was filled? Indeed, by 1853 no more bodies were buried in London churchyards. Even before that, new sources of land for burial were required. Thus, the researcher may need to seek information from crematoria or commercial cemeteries. For the capital city, you can locate these records through *Greater London Cemeteries and Crematoria* by Patricia Wolfson. Many members of the same family, bearing different surnames, may have been placed in the same purchased burial plot.

The registers of burial for the Church of England survive back to 1538. They remained substantially unaltered until 1812. The details of the person being buried were left to the discretion of whoever completed the register. The annual returns, the bishops' or archdeacons' transcripts, would be sent to the diocesan authority from about 1597. In the Diocese of Durham and the surrounding ecclesiastical jurisdictions, the amount of information recorded would have been dramatically increased if that parish used the Dade format of register, some time between 1770 and 1812 (*see* Chapter 1). If so, the date and cause of death and significant genealogical information about the deceased can be discovered. This includes, as with baptisms, the names of ancestors back to great-grandfathers of the deceased. If your ancestor died in that period, the record of burial may tell you where to look for previous generations.

Rose's Act of 1812 decreed the limited amount of information that was to be recorded. This prevented additional detail from being recorded, as the printed paper registers indicated what was to be written down about the person being buried. Only the name, date of burial, age and a very vague place of residence are likely to be found.

To locate burial registers or bishops' transcripts for a given parish, consult the usual reference sources. These would be *The Phillimore Atlas & Index of Parish Registers* edited by Cecil Humphery-Smith and *Bishops' Transcripts and Marriage Licences, Bonds and Allegations* by Jeremy Gibson.

The records will be in either the county or the diocesan record office, which can be located and visited through Jeremy Gibson and Pamela Peskett's *Records Offices: How to Find Them*. You can find and view the website for the relevant record office through *www.nationalarchives. gov.uk/archon*. Later parish registers may still remain with the incumbent of the parish. If so, they may be consulted locally by making an appointment with the custodian.

Many copies of burial records have been made. They may be indexed by surname and can be searched in either a local record office or a library. The Society of Genealogists holds copies of burial records for many parishes.

Very few cumulative indexes to the burial registers of many parishes in a given area have been produced. Where these exist, you can learn about them through *Specialist Indexes for*

Family Historians by Jeremy Gibson and Elizabeth Hampson.

Guildhall Library also holds the registers of the many English chaplaincies in Europe who chose to deposit these at home. They mainly date from the 18th and 19th centuries. For the holdings, see *The British Overseas: A Guide to Records of Births, Baptisms, Marriages, Deaths and Burials Available in the United Kingdom* by Geoffrey Yeo.

Burial records from many parishes and some cemeteries have been indexed in the *National Burial Index*, published by the Federation of Family History Societies. This is available on CD. It can be searched by surname, nationally or by county or parish.

You can pay to use the *National Burial Index* or any of the local indexes that have been collected by the Federation of Family History Societies through *www.familyhistoryonline.net*.

Nonconfirmist burials

Some chapels and other meeting places of Protestant nonconformist sects had their own burial grounds. Many others, who did not normally attend the Church of England, had to be buried in a parish graveyard, there being no alternative. The records of those buried by other denominations may have been deposited with the Registrar General at the Public Record Office in 1837. They can be searched on microfilm at the National Archives or Family Records Centre, mainly in series RG 4 to RG 6. There are indexes to some of the major nonconformist burial grounds, such as those for Gibraltar Row and Bunhill Fields. Later registers have probably remained with the church or chapel itself, although there may be copies available in the local county record office or at the Society of Genealogists. Burial records are not included in the International Genealogical Index or the British Isles Vital Records Index.

For other sects, the chances of finding burial records are varied. These may be listed in any of the specialist works on each sect published by the Society of Genealogists (*see* Chapter 1). Reference is made to them in the appropriate volume of the Society's *National Index of Parish Registers* series.

For the location of Catholic burial registers, consult Michael Gandy's *Catholic Missions and Registers 1700–1880*. Records of Quaker burials can be found through the Digests for each geographical area. Many Jewish burial grounds exist and these can be a valuable source for members of the Jewish faith. Their locations can be found in *Non-conformist, Roman Catholic, Jewish and Burial Ground Registers*. A good source of deaths and obituaries for Jews from 1871 to 1880 (as well as entries for births and marriages) is *The Jewish Victorian* edited by Doreen Berger.

Monumental inscriptions

It is always worth visiting the church or cemetery in which your ancestor was buried. The monumental inscriptions can provide a great deal more information than the individual entries recorded in the burial registers. For those laid to rest in the same grave or commemorated on the same stone, an age, and possibly an occupation, place of residence or even a place of origin, will be recorded. The relationships between them may not be stated in any other source. War memorials may also be a rich source of new information (*see* page 197). The monumental inscriptions may have been transcribed. If this was done many years ago, before acid rain, erosion and even vandalism have caused the inscription to become illegible, an earlier transcriber might have been able to decipher the inscription. Transcriptions of many gravestones in churchyards exist in libraries and county record offices. The Society of Genealogists has transcriptions of the inscriptions in

Smart data: Heraldry

The colourful study of heraldry and its records can be of great assistance to the genealogist.

A gentleman, whose right to bear a coat-of-arms was granted to him by the monarch through the heralds, could pass those armorial bearings to each of his sons. When a man married the daughter of another armiger, she might bring with her other arms which she had inherited from her own forebears. Their marriage would be represented by the impalement of the arms on one shield, the husband's arms on the left and those of his wife's father on the right. If the wife had no brothers, her arms would be joined with those of her husband to form a new coat-of-arms, which would be used by their children. The new device tells a story, through its quarterings (not just four divisions), of the families which were represented amongst the ancestors. When the person died, their arms would have been displayed outside their house or in the parish church on a hatchment made of wood and canvas.

thousands of parish churches and nonconformist graveyards. Many of them include maps or plans. Most are indexed by surname.

Do not forget the monuments inside the church. Even if your ancestor was not buried there, relatives or descendents in their home parish may commemorate their life and death.

Tombs and monuments may be found for armigerous ancestors. The coat-of-arms depicted on these is of great interest to the genealogist, because it can lead to the discovery of the surnames of families from previous generations. These can lead you to other heraldic and genealogical sources for those who were entitled to use arms (*see* Chapter 6).

Obituaries

For more important members of a community or those who had met an untimely or criminal end, a local or national newspaper may have recorded the death or burial of an ancestor. You should seek and read any obituary. It can provide hitherto unknown details of the life or relatives of the deceased. A list may be published of those attending the funeral, together with their relationships to the deceased person. This may include the names of married daughters, sisters or aunts, which would be harder to locate through other sources. A copy can be sought and made through the collections in a local library or at British Library Newspapers at Colindale, *www.bl.uk/ catalogues/newspapers.html*.

It is worth consulting the index to *The Times*. This can be achieved through *The Times Digital Archive 1785–1985* at *http://www.galeuk.com/times*. This is an institution subscription service available free of charge in some libraries, including the Family Records Centre. From the index, an image of the obituary can be displayed and copied. *The Official Index to the Times* and *Palmer's Index to the Times 1790–1905* are available online or on CD.

Deaths of servicemen may be recorded in the *London Gazette*, which is annually indexed from 1787. *The Illustrated London News*, indexed from 1731 to 1810, is also a rich source of obituaries.

In the case of armigerous ancestors, who had the right to bear a coat-of-arms, a funeral certificate, recording the names of mourners, may exist in the collections of the College of Arms; see *www.college-of-arms.gov.uk*.

Many accounts of the lives of our ancestors, recorded at their death, can be traced through published biographical sources. You can locate references to obituaries in school, college and university alumni lists or registers and in professional sources for those who were eminent in a particular trade, occupation or calling. *The Oxford Dictionary of National Biography* (online by subscription) also refers to published accounts of those who are included. Many of the principal sources were indexed by G.W. Marshall in *The Genealogists' Guide* and by J.B. Whitmore in *A Genealogical Guide: An Index to British Pedigrees in Continuation of Marshall's Genealogists' Guide*. This will lead us to printed obituaries and records of burials of ancestors in serial publications such as *The Gentleman's Magazine* and *Musgrave's Obituaries*.

Probate records

After the death of an ancestor, his or her temporal estate may have been brought to the attention of a probate authority. If so, seek documentation that will determine what became of their possessions, both real and personal. This assumes that it has not been destroyed by a later catastrophe, such as bombing during World War II. For instance, bombs destroyed most probate material in some dioceses of the West Country.

If the person left a will, the executor(s) was responsible for ensuring that the last wishes of the deceased were carried out. To this end, they may have taken the will to the local probate authority where, following its ratification as a legal document, it would be proved and probate granted. You can then find the original will or, more likely, an office copy, to read how your ancestor wanted to bequeath their property. You should remember that many other wills were made and dealt with by the family of the deceased, but were never formally registered with the probate court. If so, the chances of it having survived for research are much smaller.

If no will was made, someone may have requested or applied for the power to deal with the person's estate. An administration (or admon) would then be granted by the court to appoint an administrator. This would be a relative, a creditor, a solicitor or even the state. The estate could then be divided based on the law of intestate succession as it stood at that time. In other cases, a form of will may have existed but not been legal for some reason. Perhaps an executor was not named or had died before the testator. The will may not have been dated or signed. If so, the deficient or unacceptable will could still be taken as a guide to the deceased's wishes and could be annexed to the grant of administration.

It is worth looking for any probate documents for a forebear or relative to extract their genealogical content. Just as in the case of monumental inscriptions, they can reveal relationships which cannot be determined from isolated entries in parish registers or certificates of birth, marriage or death. Any possible testator in the family should be considered as a new and potentially rich source of new clues. Maiden aunts, who had no descendents of their own to whom to leave their treasured possessions, are notoriously valuable recorders of distant relatives and interrelationships. Do not just look for wills of those with one particular surname but look for relatives with other surnames. Remember that the mother's relatives are just as likely to leave bequests to grandchildren, nephews and cousins as are those of the direct paternal line.

From 1858, the process of probate became the responsibility of the state. Before that date, the documents may be found in any one of a number of ecclesiastical and civil courts in varying levels of hierarchy. This makes the process of finding the will, administration or any other surviving documents – or a statement that they once existed but have since perished – a highly intriguing hunt.

Wills after 1858

There has been only one main authority that has proved wills and granted administrations since 1858. This makes the act of searching for probate documents relatively straightforward. The main source is the national annual indexes for England and Wales, which can be searched at the Principal Registry of the Family Division, known as the Principal Probate Registry. The indexes can be searched to the present date. Note that there are separate indexes to wills and administrations from 1858 to 1870. After that, they are mixed together alphabetically. Microfiche copies of the indexes are available for research at the Family Records Centre to 1943.

The brief abstract of the grant of probate or administration is valuable in identifying an individual before a copy is obtained. The probate indexes give addresses, occupations, marital status and date of death. They are much more informative than the indexes to deaths and provide a method of discriminating between those who had a common combination of forename and surname. As they are annual, they are less taxing to search than the equivalent quarterly indexes of death before 1984.

The occupation of the deceased is usually shown in the indexes from 1858 to 1922. The name of the person dealing with the estate can often be an identifiable relative. Unfortunately, from 1968 to 1995 the name of the executor or administrator is not included in the indexes. Wills and admons may be included for those who died abroad but had estates in England and Wales. Their deaths will be more difficult to find without the information recorded in the indexes.

A copy of a will or administration costs very little. It can be available within one hour. If you want it to be sealed for legal purposes, it can be collected after five working days or will be posted to you.

Wills before 1858

It is a much more complex process to locate all probate documents for your ancestors and their relatives before 1858. Any one of several courts in a hierarchy of probate authorities could have dealt with the estate you seek. In general, for all parishes of England and Wales there would have been, in ascending order of importance, an archdeaconry court (under the jurisdiction of an archdeacon), a Consistory or Commissary Court (the court of a bishop) and one or two Prerogative Courts (those of the archbishops) depending on whether the person had property in the north or south of the country (or both). In addition, there were other authorities that could deal with probate matters – for instance, Peculiar or manorial courts. Overall, there were courts of appeal, such as the High Court of Delegates and the Court of Arches. The courts of Chancery, Exchequer and Judicature (*see* Chapter 5) also heard matters associated with probate.

If there was property in more than one archdeaconry or diocese, or there was a dispute over the inheritance, the case might have been elevated to a higher court than would have been expected. In general, the will or administration of a labourer, if it merited such attention, would be found in the records of an archdeaconry court. That of a lord of the manor, gentleman or noble, would be proved by the Prerogative Court of Canterbury or York and the estates of those of intermediate rank or profession would be found in the courts of the bishop. However, this is not always the case. You should search the calendars and indexes to the records of all courts that could have been involved. No stone should be left unturned. Indeed, during the Commonwealth Interregnum, from about 1640 to 1660, as most ecclesiastical authorities had been suspended, even the wills of labourers were dealt with by the Prerogative Court of Canterbury. If your ancestor was a serviceman, try the separate collections of military wills at the National Archives (*see* Chapter 4).

Besides wills and administrations, there may

be other documents, such as inventories, listings of the goods, chattels and debts of the deceased, or curation and tuition bonds to ensure the care and education of children of the deceased during their minority. In some courts, all papers relating to a person's estate are stored or filed together. In others, they are separated, with original wills, act book copies, inventories and bonds being given different class, series or catalogue numbers. You must find, order and read each document to discover the whole story of the division of the estate. *Wills and Other Probate Records* by K. Grannum and N. Taylor will help with this search.

The Phillimore Atlas & Index of Parish Registers edited by Cecil Humphery-Smith provides a pictorial representation of the ecclesiastical court system. However, it is sometimes misleading about each of the two lower levels of jurisdiction, those of the archdeacon and bishop of that area. There will always be one court at each level for every parish. Make sure that the wills and administrations of all levels are searched. For example, for those who lived in Leicestershire, the Archdeaconry of Leicester was the lowest level of probate court. It is clear that the Prerogative Court of Canterbury was the highest authority. *The Atlas* does not show the intermediate-level court, in this case the Consistory Court of Lincoln. If you do not use the records of that court too, you will have missed a whole collection of probate documents for inhabitants of that area.

This is made clear in Jeremy Gibson and Else Churchill's *Probate Jurisdictions: Where to Look for Wills*. Used in conjunction with maps in *The Atlas*, this will lead you to all relevant courts. You will discover where their records are held and the finding aids to help in locating and ordering the documents. There will be card or manuscript calendars or indexes in the diocesan record office. You should also use any published, CD-ROM or online indexes. The Society of Genealogists holds copies of many of these indexes and calendars from around the country. The Family Records Centre also holds a selection of printed indexes to probate records. Not all finding aids will be to both wills and administrations. Other documents may be included or remain accessible only through calendars in the search room.

The online index to the wills proved by the Prerogative Court of Canterbury, *www. national archives.gov.uk/documentsonline*, now allows a rapid search in the records of that court in series PROB 11. You can limit your search, if needed, to those with a certain name who lived in a particular county or parish. You can choose only those with a given occupation or whose will was proved in a particular century. This search is free at the Family Records Centre or the National Archives. A fee is charged for access online.

Since this court was responsible for those who lived abroad, especially in British colonies, it can be a very important source of information and, in some cases, proof for those who live in modern America and who are descended from emigrants to those shores before Independence.

Inland Revenue and Estate Duty

From 1796, tax was imposed on probate estates. For the collection of the payments due, copies of wills and administrations were sent to London to the Inland Revenue. Only estates over a certain value were subject to the tax. The lower limit for taxation was increased several times over the 19th century. Tax was not levied when the heirs were close family members. The degree of exempt relationships became much narrower as time went by. Thus, not all estates will be found in this collection.

The microfilm indexes to the Inland Revenue or Estate Duty wills and administrations are in IR 27 at the National Archives or Family Records

Centre. The synopsis records of the probate accounts are in IR 26. These show the name and occupation of the deceased, where he or she lived, the date of the will or administration, the value of the estate, the name of the executor(s) or administrators(s) and their place(s) of residence. The date it was registered and the name of the probate court are recorded. Details of the heirs, including their relationship to the deceased, and the tax payable are laid out.

If the bequests were payable only when the beneficiary reached a given age or at marriage, the Inland Revenue would need to keep track of the estate, perhaps for many years. The annotations in the accounts (available on microfilm at the National Archives or Family Records Centre to 1858) can often provide the date at which an heir reached a certain age, the date of their marriage and, in the case of daughters, their new married surname. The very small additions, often hidden among internal file and case numbers and annotations, may record when people died or if they were alive at a given important date from the standpoint of the Revenue.

Many of these clues will not be recorded in the original will. If the IR 26 accounts are not examined, a wealth of genealogical information can be missed. The clues found can be pursued through the indexes of civil registration or census returns. It must be stressed that the accounts, being available from 1796 to 1903, are also available for wills and administrations to be found in the first 46 years of the records held at the Principal Probate Registry. You can examine the accounts for post-1858 probate estates, now called Succession or Estate Duty Registers, at the National Archives at Kew. They need to be ordered in advance.

If the court that proved a will or granted an administration is not known, the Inland Revenue collection can provide an invaluable method of finding documents from 1812 onwards. From 1812, all wills are found in one annual index for each year in IR 27, irrespective of the court which proved the document. These indexes can be used to locate the estate accounts and determine the court that proved the will. Once you have established the name of the court, you can go to those records and obtain a copy of the will. For administrations, all documents are indexed together except for those granted by the Prerogative Court of Canterbury.

The National Archivist website, *www.national archivist.com*, provides a pay-for-view annual index to all administrations and wills from 1796 to the late 19th century, and so is useful for the pre-1812 period. There is also a searchable index to the accounts for County Court Wills and Administrations (not Prerogative Court of Canterbury) from 1796 to 1811 at *www.national archives.gov.uk/documentsonline*. The images of the accounts can be viewed.

The collection of wills and administrations sent to the Inland Revenue for the collection of death duty was largely destroyed. However, the copies of the wills for the first half of the 19th century were returned to those dioceses which had lost their documents during the bombing in World War II. Some of the documents destroyed in that catastrophe were replaced. Thus, even for those areas, some probate records survive to tell us more about the possessions and relationships of our ancestors.

Smart reading on death records

Bishops' Transcripts and Marriage Licences, Bonds and Allegations, by Jeremy Gibson, 5th edn (Federation of Family History Societies, 2001)

The British Overseas: A Guide to Records of Births, Baptisms, Marriages, Deaths and Burials Available in the United Kingdom, by Geoffrey Yeo, revised by Philippa Smith, 3rd edn (Guildhall Library, 1994)

Catholic Missions and Registers 1700–1880, by Michael Gandy (Society of Genealogists, 1993)

Coroners' Records in England and Wales, by Jeremy Gibson and Colin Rodgers, 2nd edn (Federation of Family History Societies, 2000)

A Genealogical Guide: An Index to British Pedigrees in Continuation of Marshall's Genealogists' Guide, by J.B. Whitmore (Walford, 1953)

The Genealogists' Guide, by G.W. Marshall, 4th edn (reprint, Genealogical Publishing, 1903)

Greater London Cemeteries and Crematoria, by Patricia Wolfson, revised by Cliff Webb, 6th edn (Society of Genealogists, 1999)

The International Vital Records Handbook, by Thomas Jay Kemp, 4th edn (Genealogical Publishing, 2000)

The Jewish Victorian, edited by Doreen Berger (Robert Boyd, 1999)

National Burial Index, 2nd edn (Federation of Family History Societies, 2004)

Non-conformist, Roman Catholic, Jewish and Burial
    Ground Registers, 3rd edn (Guildhall Library,
    2002)

The Official Index to the Times

The Oxford Dictionary of National Biography (Oxford
    University Press, 2004; also available as an online
    subscription)

Palmer's Index to the Times 1790–1905 (Chadwyck-
    Healey, ongoing)

The Phillimore Atlas & Index of Parish Registers, by
    Cecil Humphery-Smith, 3rd edn (Phillimore, 2003)

Probate Jurisdictions: Where to Look for Wills, by
    Jeremy Gibson and Else Churchill, 5th edn
    (Federation of Family History Societies, 2002)

Records Offices: How to Find Them, by Jeremy Gibson
    and Pamela Peskett, 9th edn (Federation of Family
    History Societies, 2002)

Specialist Indexes for Family Historians, by Jeremy
    Gibson and Elizabeth Hampson, 2nd edn
    (Federation of Family History Societies, 2000)

Wills and Other Probate Records, by K. Grannum and
    N. Taylor (The National Archives, 2004)

Toggle graphic version | Site Map

General Register Office
for
SCOTLAND
Information about Scotland's people

Registering
150 years of Scottish life

You are in: Home >

Information about Scotland's People

The General Register Office for Scotland (GROS) is the department of the devolved Scottish Administration responsible for the registration of births, marriages, deaths, divorces, and adoptions in Scotland. We are responsible for the Census which we use, with other sources of information, to produce population and household statistics. We make available important information for family history.

Registration >

How to register a birth or death, or get married in Scotland, order birth, death or marriage certificates, get information on adoption and more...

Your History >

Open the door to researching your family history

Population Statistics >

Home
Registration
Statistics
Family Records
News
About Us
Contact Us

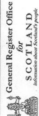

The Census >
Explore and understand the Census and plan the future...

Census Results >
Use, explore and understand the full potential of Census output...

ScotlandsPeople >
The online source of civil registration, open

Search
enter keywords   go >

What do you want to do?
Find out how to...
go >

Did you know?
Households consisting of two or more adults with children are projected to decrease from 21% of all households in 2002 to 15% by 2016.

What's new
View recent additions to the GROS website...

Future publications
Find out which publications we plan to release in the future...

Chapter 8

Exploring further

- Scotland
- Ireland
- Searching further
- The internet

Although this book concentrates on finding out about ancestors in England and Wales, you may trace your ancestors back to Scotland or Ireland. The family may have come from there or forebears may have moved north of the border or across the Irish Sea in the course of their work. The records of these two separate areas of the British Isles may include important evidence about part of your family's history.

Scotland

The records of Scotland are in some ways better and more informative than the genealogical sources used for ancestral research in England or Wales, but in other ways they are less complete. There are also additional sources that can be used. Most of the sources used frequently by genealogists are centralized in Edinburgh.

Registration of births, marriages and deaths began in 1855, 18 years later than the system in England and Wales. In that first year, an impressive amount of information was recorded, especially about those who were born or died. If your ancestor, or one of their close relatives, was recorded in 1855, that document will provide a wealth of clues to the wider family history.

After 1855, the data to be registered was reduced considerably but still exceeds that in the equivalent documents south of the border. A birth certificate usually includes the date and place of marriage of the parents. The marriage certificate gives the names of both the father and the mother of the bride and the groom, and whether they were alive or dead at the time that their son or daughter married. A death registration provides the names of the deceased's parents, if known to the informant, and the deceased's spouse, if married. The identification of the parentage of an elderly person who died after 1855 would be particularly useful when seeking that person's baptism, which may have been in the late 18th century.

Since it is not necessary to order certified copies of vital certificates from the records of civil registration in Scotland (General Register Office for Scotland), this allows the researcher immediate access to the genealogical information needed to proceed to the next step in the research. It really may be possible to do your family tree in one day!

The indexes and records of birth to 1905, marriage to 1930 and death to as late as 1955 can be searched and copied for a small fee online through *www.scotlandspeople.gov.uk*.

This site also provides access to the indexes and images of the Scottish censuses and the Old Parochial Registers. In general, the parish registers survive from a much later date and are far less informative than those of England. Many only date from the 18th century and often there are no records of death or burial.

Other sources such as probate records, deeds and land records are held at the National Archives of Scotland. A free index to Scottish testaments (probate records bequeathing personal property) from 1513 to 1901 can be searched through the Scotland's People site.

The records of Scottish servicemen are mainly in the National Archives at Kew in England.

Ireland

The records of Ireland are far less complete than those for other parts of the British Isles. Many were not properly kept or have been lost through government or civil action. This can make the search for the native Irish very frustrating. Much more information will be found about the Anglo-Irish who owned much of the land and lived in the large houses.

Registration of births, marriages and deaths were centrally recorded for all from 1864. (Non-

Catholic marriages were registered by the state from 1845.) These can be searched through the national indexes in the search room in the General Register Office in Dublin. Access can also be achieved from the General Register Office of Northern Ireland in Belfast. It is not necessary to obtain certified copies for genealogical research. You can obtain a photocopy of the entry which will allow you to search for the next generation during the same visit. Their format is identical to those of England and Wales.

Only the census returns for 1901 and 1911 survive in their entirety. These usually only record the county of birth. The absence of the parish of origin makes it very difficult to move on to search for a baptism of the person in the appropriate registers.

In Ireland, it is very important to know the religion of the family. There are separate registers recording baptisms and marriages for those who attended the Church of Ireland or the Catholic Church. In the north of Ireland, your ancestors may also have been Presbyterian, especially if they had strong links with Scotland. Many registers are incomplete and often lack burial entries, especially for Catholics, or may have been lost. Many remain in the care of the incumbent or the parish priest. There may be copies in the appropriate repositories in Dublin or Belfast. There are also local projects to index them through heritage centres, based on a county or a diocese.

Most probate records and other important sources, such as marriage licences, were destroyed in 1922. Some had been abstracted before their loss. These will enable the genealogist to learn some of the information that was originally included despite the fact that the document no longer exists. Other sources, such as Griffith's Valuation of Ireland and the information used in making claims for old age pensions from 1908 to 1922, may replace, to some extent, those important records which were destroyed. Sources for those employed by the state, such as servicemen, police, coastguards and customs men, will be in London at the National Archives.

It will still prove very difficult to trace a Catholic family back into the 18th century.

Searching further

If you have come across a problem in your search for information about, for example, a particular surname, make contact with someone else who may be able to help you.

Smart data: Keeping track of the internet

The huge variety of resources now available to internet family historians makes for a rich online experience, but also for a potentially confusing one. It is a good idea to have a reliable published guide to hand, by your side, as you surf the net. One of the best is Peter Christian's 'bible', *The Genealogist's Internet* (3rd edition, 2005), published by the National Archives, which has a coverage that is both broad and deep. Scotland and Ireland, as well as countries overseas, are discussed in addition to England and Wales. You can then annotate and personalize your guide as new websites of interest to you emerge, or as web addresses change.

You can find other genealogists who may be researching the same problem through the *Genealogical Research Directory* edited by Keith Johnson and Malcolm Sainty. Published annually since 1982, each edition includes a new list of researchers and their addresses. You may find someone on the other side of the world who is also interested in your problem. They may have leads to other clues and documents. The Federation of Family History Societies produces the British Isles Genealogical Register on microfiche.

That can lead you to those who are interested in the same family.

Should you be researching a rare surname, see if someone is already collecting all references to those who had that name and its variants. They can advertise their lifetime's obsession by joining the Guild of One-Name Studies. The surnames that they are studying and their address are listed at *www.one-name.org*.

The internet

If you surf the internet, you could find someone who has the vital clue to help with your research. There are now a huge number of message boards and mailing lists to be contacted. Probably the best access point is through *www.cyndislist. com/mailing.htm*. You can find and visit sites that are relevant to your particular need or problem.

The largest collection is on Rootsweb.com and this can be browsed using *http://lists. rootsweb.com* for mailing lists relating to many specific surnames, geographical areas and topics. You can find the archive of each mailing list at *http://archiver.rootsweb.com*. This can be searched by subject or chronologically. Message boards at *http://boards.ancestry.com* allow you to contact other researchers to pose and answer questions about a particular surname, topic or place.

You may even want to try to contact other relatives through *www.genesreunited.com* or *www.lostcousins.com*. They may have information or documents which will help you to overcome that apparently insurmountable obstacle.

Remember, do not be deterred if at first you do not succeed – just keep trying. Leave no source unused, no document unread, no website untried and no clue uninvestigated. The answer may be out there somewhere!

Useful addresses
record offices and libraries

British Library
96 Euston Road
London NW12DB
Tel. 020 7412 7332
www.bl.uk

British Library Newspapers
Colindale Avenue
London NW9 5HE
Tel. 020 7412 7393
ww.bl.uk/catalogues/newspapers.html

Catholic Central Library
(currently between premises)
contact:
167 Waller Road
London SE14 5LX
Tel. 020 7732 8379
www.catholic-library.org.uk

Catholic Record Society
12 Melbourne Place
Wolsingham
County Durham DL13 3EH
Tel. 01388 527747
www.catholic-history.org.uk/crs

Church of Jesus Christ of Latter-day Saints (Mormons)
Hyde Park Family History Centre
64–68 Exhibition Road
South Kensington
London SW7 2PA
Tel. 020 7589 8561
www.familysearch.org

College of Arms
Queen Victoria Street
London EC4V 4BT
Tel. 020 7248 2762
www.college-of-arms.gov.uk

Commonwealth War Graves Commission
2 Marlow Road
Maidenhead
Berkshire SL6 7DX
Tel. 01628 634221
www.cwgc.org

Corporation of London Records Office
See London Metropolitan Archives
www.cityoflondon.gov.uk/archives/clro

County Record Offices
for addresses consult:
R. Blatchford, *The Family and Local History Handbook* (Robert Blatchford Publishing, updated annually)

or J. Gibson and P. Peskett,
Record Offices: How to Find Them,
9th edn (Federation of
Family History Societies, 2002)
www.nationalarchives.gov.uk/archon/

Diocesan Record Offices
for localities consult:
J. Gibson, *Bishops' Transcripts and Marriage
Licences, Bonds and Allegations*, 5th edn
(Federation of Family History Societies,
2001) (then see CRO above)

Family Records Centre
1 Myddelton Street
London EC1R 1UW
Tel. 020 8392 5300
www.familyrecords.gov.uk/frc

Federation of Family History Societies
PO Box 2425
Coventry CV5 6YX
www.ffhs.org.uk

Religious Society of Friends (Quakers)
Friends' House
173–177 Euston Road
London NW1 2BJ
Tel. 020 7663 1135
www.quaker.org.uk

General Register Office (for Ireland)
Joyce House
8–11 Lombard Street East
Dublin 2
Eire
Tel. 00353 1 635 4000
www.groireland.ie

General Register Office for Northern Ireland
Oxford House
49–55 Chichester Street
Belfast BT1 4HL
Tel. 028 90 252000
www.groni.gov.uk

General Register Office for Scotland
New Register House
3 West Register Street
Edinburgh EH1 3YT
Tel. 0131 314 4433
www.gro-scotland.gov.uk

The General Registry (of the Isle of Man)
Isle of Man Courts of Justice
Deemster's Walk
Bucks Road
Douglas
Isle of Man IM1 3AR
Tel. 01624 685250
www.gov.im/registries

Guildhall Library
Aldermanbury
London EC2P 2EJ
Tel. 020 7332 1863
www.cityoflondon.gov.uk/guildhalllibrary

Her Majesty's Greffier
The Royal Court House
St Peter Port
Guernsey GY1 2PB
Tel. 01481 725277

Judicial Greffe
Royal Square
10 Royal Street
St Helier
Jersey JE2 4WA
Tel. 01534 502335
www.gov.je/judicialgreffe

House of Lords Record Office
The Clerk of the Records
Parliamentary Archives
London SW1A 0PW
Tel. 020 7219 3074
www.parliament.uk

The Institute of Heraldic and Genealogical Studies
79–82 Northgate
Canterbury
Kent CT1 1BA
Tel. 01227 768664
www.ihgs.ac.uk

London Metropolitan Archives
40 Northampton Road
London EC1R 0HB
Tel. 020 7332 3820
www.cityoflondon.gov.uk/lma

Ministry of Defence
Army Personnel Centre
Historical Disclosures
Mailpoint 400
Kentigern House
65 Brown Street
Glasgow G2 8EX
Tel. 0141 224 3515
www.mod.uk/contacts/army_records.htm

The National Archives
Kew
Richmond
Surrey TW9 4DU
Tel. 020 8876 3444
www.nationalarchives.gov.uk

National Archives of Scotland
HM General Register House
2 Princes Street
Edinburgh EH1 3YY
Tel. 0131 535 1314
www.nas.gov.uk

National Library of Wales
Aberystwyth
Ceredigion
Wales SY23 3BU
Tel. 01970 632800
www.llgc.org.uk

Navy Search
TNT Archive Services
Tetron Point
William Nadin Way
Swadlincote
Derbyshire DE11 0BB
Tel. 01283 227912
www.mod.uk/contacts/rn_records.htm

Principal Registry of the Family Division
Probate Department
First Avenue House
42–49 High Holborn
London WC1V 6NP
Tel. 020 7947 7000
www.hmcourtservice.gov.uk

RAF (IM1b)
Room 5
Building 248A
RAF Personnel Management Agency
RAF Innsworth
Gloucester GL3 1EZ
www.mod.uk/contacts/raf_records.htm

Royal Marines
The Historical Records Office
DPS(N)2
Building 1/152
Victory View
PP 36
HMNB Portsmouth
West Sussex PO1 3PX
Tel. 02392 727531
www.mod.uk/contacts/rm_records.htm

Society of Genealogists
14 Charterhouse Buildings
Goswell Road
London EC1M 7BA
Tel. 020 7251 8799
www.sog.org.uk

Useful websites

General

www.a2a.org.uk Access to Archives website. Links to catalogues of record offices, archives and libraries. Database searchable by name to wide range of collections.

www.ancestry.co.uk Subscription access to huge collection of databases.

www.ancestry.com British Isles and world including civil registration indexes, census indexes, parish registers and indexes and many other sources.

www.britishorigins.com Pay-for-view access to many important databases for British Isles.

www.cyndislist.com Worldwide site for finding information about sources, archives and researchers.

www.familyhistoryonline.net Pay-for-view access to a series of databases collected by the Federation of Family History Societies, especially to census and parish register indexes. Free access to 1881 census surname index.

www.familyrecords.gov.uk Provides links to websites of other major archives and record offices in UK

www.familysearch.org Site of the Church of Jesus Christ of Latter-day Saints, which includes the International Genealogical Index, Ancestral File and Pedigree Resource File and index to 1881 census. Access to the library catalogue showing the largest worldwide collection of genealogical sources.

www.genuki.org.uk Gateway site to sources for research in UK. Links to record offices, libraries and sources for each county and region.

www.nationalarchives.gov.uk The National Archives
website for 1901 census index, PCC wills, World
War I medal rolls, whereabouts of hospital records,
manorial documents register, soldiers' documents,
The National Archives catalogue and surname
searches, Archon, information leaflets and much
more.

www.sog.org.uk Society of Genealogists' website.
Access to catalogue of largest collection of
genealogical material for Britain in this country.

www.scotlandspeople.gov.uk Access to births,
marriages and deaths, census returns and parish
registers for Scotland.

Civil registration indexes

www.1837online.com Pay-for-view site for online
access to GRO indexes.

www.ancestry.co.uk Subscription access to GRO
indexes.

www.bmdindex.co.uk Pay-for-view site for online access
to GRO indexes.

www.familyrelatives.org Pay-for-view site for online
access to GRO indexes.

www.freebmd.org.uk Free partial index to GRO indexes
for 19th century.

www.gro.gov.uk GRO's own website including online
ordering of certificates.

www.ukbmd.org.uk Links to records and indexes of
local register offices in UK.

Censuses

www.1837online.com Pay-for-view index to 1861
census.

www.1901censusonline.com Access to national 1901
census index

www.ancestry.co.uk Subscription access to national
    surname indexes for 1861 to 1901 censuses.
www.britishorigins.com Partial pay-for-view index to
    1841 census.
www.familysearch.org Free index to 1881 census.
www.freecen.org.uk Free online access to growing
    collection of census indexes.

Other sources

www.cwgc.org Commonwealth War Graves
    Commission free searchable database of those who
    died as a result of conflict.
www.ellisisland.org Passengers to USA 1892–1924.
www.freereg.org.uk Free online index to growing
    collection of entries from parish registers.
www.historicaldirectories.org Online trade and
    commercial directories.
www.oldbaileyonline.org.uk Free index and abstracts of
    trial records at Old Bailey 1674–1799.
www.workhouses.org.uk Information about
    workhouses.

Further reading

General reading

A. Adolph, *Tracing your Family History* (Collins, 2004)

J. Cole and J. Titford, *Tracing Your Family Tree* (Countryside Books, 2004)

M. Herber, *Ancestral Trails* (Sutton, 2004)

D. Hey, *Journeys in Family History* (The National Archives, 2004)

Reader's Digest, *Explore Your Family's Past* (Reader's Digest, 2000)

Other topics

A. Bevan, *Tracing Your Ancestors in the Public Record Office* (Public Record Office, 2002)

P. Christian, *The Genealogist's Internet* (The National Archives, 2004)

S. Colwell, *Dictionary of Genealogical Sources in the Public Record Office* (Weidenfeld and Nicolson, 1992)

S. Colwell, *The Family Records Centre* (Public Record Office, 2002)

S. Friar, *Heraldry for the Local Historian and Genealogist* (Sutton, 1996)

E. Higgs, *Making Sense of the Census Revisited* (University of London, 2005)

S. Lumas, *Making Use of the Census* (The National Archives, 2004)

See also the 'Smart reading' sections at the end of chapters 1–7.

Index

Access to Archives (A2A) 9
adoption 29–30
Aldous, V.E. 174
Annal, David 9
The Apprentices of Great Britain
    67
apprenticeships 66–70, 72–3
armed services 4, 14, 25, 112–13,
    130–2, 214; *see also specific
    branches*
Army 4, 113–22
Assize Courts 137, 138, 140,
    141–3
Attestation and Discharge Papers
    114, 120

banns book 97–8
baptism 14, 16, 26, 32, 34–5, 92,
    156–7
Barrington, Rev 38
bastardy warrants 55–7
Berger, Doreen 205
Bernau Index 151
Bevan, Amanda 27, 90
birth indexes 16–18, 30–4
birth records 14, 16, 18, 43–4,
    58–9, 78; abroad 24–9; non-
    conformists 43, 45–6; place of
    17–18, 31; Scotland 227;
    websites 23
bishops' transcripts 40–1, 42–3
Boyd's Inhabitants of London 176
Boyd's London Burial Index 94

Boyd's Marriage Index 92–3, 94
British Genealogical Bibliographies
    70, 181
British Isles Genealogical Register
    231
British Isles Vital Records Index
    46, 52, 92
British Library 25–6, 89, 178, 198
British Library Newspapers 143,
    207–9
British Origins Database 70
burials 200–5
Business Archives Council 185

Cambridge University 64
Canterbury, Archbishop of 100–1
Catholics 46–7, 204, 229–30
census indexes 15, 103–8
census records 5, 14–15, 48,
    102–3, 228
Central Criminal Court 142
Chancery 149–52, 214
Channel Islands 27–8, 198
Chapman, Colin 63, 157
Chester, Palatinate of 141–2,
    180
Christian, Peter 231
Church of England 34, 35–7, 92,
    201
Church of Ireland 229
Church of Jesus Christ of Latter-
    day Saints 9, 44, 46, 48, 50–1,
    104, 114–15, 155

Churchill, E. 216
Citizens of London (Boyd) 94, 176
city directories 162–3
*City Livery Companies and
    Related Organisations* 64, 69
The Clergy List 183
coat-of-arms 177–8, 206
College of Arms 178, 208
commercial directories 162–5
Commissary Court 213
Commonwealth War Graves
    Commission 121, 197–8
confiscation of land 151, 170–1
Consistory Court 213, 216
Coroners' Records in England 194
Corporation of London Record
    Office 71
county directories 163–4
county record offices 36, 80, 81
Court Baron 146–8
Court Leet 146–8
Court of Arches 214
criminal courts 140
Criminal Registers 143–4
Crockford's Clerical Directory 40,
    183

Dade registers 37–8, 201
death indexes 18, 21, 31–2
death registration 192–200,
    222–3, 227
Deed Poll 20
Dell, Alan 128, 172
diaries 120
DiNardo, R.L. 125
Diocesan and Prerogative Courts
    98
diocesan record offices 56, 157–8
divorce 101–2
Durham, Bishop of 38
Durham, Palatinate of 141, 180

ecclesiastical court 156–8
Education Act (1870) 62, 63
education records 14, 62–4, 65,
    75
electoral rolls 165–6
elopement 82, 88
employment records 14, 180–5,
    186–8
England and Wales 14–15, 16–18,
    29–30, 192–7
equity courts 148–52
estate duty 217–20
Exchequer 149–52, 167–8, 214

Faculty Office 100–1
Family Bibles 14
Family History Centres 9
family history societies 96
Family Records Centre 16;
    adoption 29–30; army records
    115–16; birth records 27, 30,
    45–6; census indexes 106;
    electoral rolls 166; General
    Register Office 25; marriages
    90; national indexes 19, 23;
    non-conformists 49; Research
    Guides 8
FamilySearch website 49, 51
Federation of Family History
    Societies 8, 52, 70, 104, 203,
    231
Foster, Joseph 182, 183
Fowler, S. 119
freemen 71, 173–5

Gandy, Michael 47, 204
genealogical magazines 7–8
Genealogists' Guides 179
General Register Offices 25, 30,
    195, 197; Belfast 229–30;
    Dublin 229–30; Scotland 227

Gibraltar 28
Gibson, Jeremy 39, 40, 52, 70,
    73, 96, 100, 106, 113, 128, 129,
    141, 156, 166, 169, 172, 181,
    194, 202, 203, 216
Grannum, K. 215
Griffith's Valuation of Ireland 230
Guild of One-Name Studies 232
Guildhall Library 28, 69, 71, 90,
    142, 174, 175, 182, 199
guilds 62, 68–71

Hampson, Elizabeth 52, 70, 96,
    106, 113, 181, 203
Hardwicke, Lord 79, 91
Harleian Society 179
Hawkings, David 145
Healey, Chadwyck 142
Hearth Tax 139, 168–9
Henry VIII 35
heraldry 5, 177–80, 207
High Court of Delegates 214
Horwitz, H. 149
House of Lords Record Office
    171–2
Huguenot Society 173
Humphery-Smith, Cecil 36, 178,
    202, 215

illegitimacy 14, 54–7, 137, 154,
    157
The Illusrated London News 208
immigrants 173
Imperial War Museum 120
Index Ecclesiasticus 183
India 83, 88, 89, 198
Inland Revenue 217–20
inquisitions post mortem 5
Institute of Heraldic and
    Genealogic Studies 94, 98
inter-library loans 8–9

International Genealogical Index
    44, 48–50, 92
International Memoranda 28, 90,
    199
International Vital Records
    Handbook 90
internet 7, 22–4, 85–8, 231, 232–3
inventories 215
Ireland 15, 27, 198, 228–30
Ireland, Northern 27, 198, 229–30

Jacobs, P.M. 65
Jewish Genealogical Society 48
Jews 91–2, 173, 205
Johnson, Keith 231

Kemp, Thomas Jay 29, 199
Kitzmiller, J.M. 116

Lambeth Palace Library 100
Lancaster, Duchy of 180
Land Tax 169–70
Lay Subsidies 167
Leicester University 164
London 68, 70–1, 142
London Gazette 118, 125, 208
London Metropolitan Archives 71,
    142, 175
lying-in hospitals 49

Man, Isle of 27
manorial courts 144, 145–8, 213
Manorial Documents Register
    148
Markham, William 38
marriage 7, 20, 78–83, 91–2,
    97–101
Marriage Act (1753) 79, 91
marriage certificates 43, 53, 78,
    80–1, 83–90, 98–100, 109, 227
marriage indexes 92–7

Marshall, G.W. 209
Marshall, J. 125
Medlycott, Mervyn 129, 169
merchant companies 68–71
Metropolitan Wesleyan Registry 46
militia 128–9
Milligan, E.H. 47
Ministry of Defence 114, 123, 128
monumental inscriptions 205–6
Moore, Susan T. 150
Munk, W. 182

names: changing of 17, 20–1, 23; common 3, 4, 17, 21, 33; internet searches 232–3; localizing 53; spelling 18–19, 86–7, 107; women's 7, 20, 23, 194
National Archives 8, 219–20; The Apprentices of Great Britain 67; army records 114–18; birth records 45–6; Chancery 150; divorce 102; marriages 90; military wills 214; National Register of Archives 185; naturalization 172–3; non-conformists 49; pay-for-view census index 104; pedigree rolls 179–80; professional records 182
National Burial Index 203
National Index of Parish Registers 37, 204
National Library of Wales 142
National Roll of the Great War 121–2
naval dockyards 124
Navy Lists 125; see also Royal Navy
newspapers 143

non-conformists 34, 43–6, 79, 151, 203–5
Non-Statutory Returns 198–9

oaths 171–2
obituaries 192, 205, 206–7, 209
O'Byrne, W.R. 125
Old Bailey 142
Old Parochial Registers 228
Overseers of the Poor 55, 67, 72, 154
Oxford Dictionary of National Biography 183–4, 208–9
Oxford University 64

Pallot's Baptism Index 52, 96
Pallot's Marriage Index 93–6
Pappalardo, B. 126, 127
parish church records 39–40
parish officials 152–6
parish priests 47
parish registers 36, 40–1, 42–3, 100
Park, Peter 146
Peculiar court 213
pedigree rolls 5, 177, 179–80
pensions 116–17, 124
Peskett, Pamela 39, 202
The Phillimore Atlas & Index of Parish Registers 36, 53–4, 92, 202, 215–16
Phillimore Marriage Register 93–4
poll books 165–6
Poll Taxes 167
Poor Law 5, 56, 72–3, 137, 152–6
Poor Law Unions 79, 155, 156
Prerogative Court 213, 214, 215, 216, 219
prisons 143–4
probate records 192, 209–12
Probert, Eric 185

professional records 14, 180–5, 186–8
Protestation Returns 171–2
Public Record Office 26, 204

Quakers 44, 47, 91–2
Quarter Sessions 56, 72–3, 137, 138–41, 140, 168–9

Raymond, Stuart 70, 71, 180–1
Recusant Rolls 151
regiments 89, 113, 115–16
Registrar General 16, 19, 44, 80, 81, 204
Requests court 151–2
Research Guides 8
Reynard, Keith 185
Rogers, Colin 156, 166, 194
Rose's Act 35, 38, 201–2
Royal Air Force 122–3
Royal Marines 127–8
Royal Navy 68, 123–8
Ruvigny, Marquis de 121

Sainty, Malcolm 231
School, University and College Registers 65–6
Scotland 14–15, 27, 198, 226–8
sequestration 170–1
service records: see armed services
Sharpe, Hilary 151
Sims, R. 179
Smith, Philippa 28
Society of Genealogists 37, 42, 44, 65–7, 106, 176–7, 182, 202, 204
Spencer, W. 119, 123, 129
Star Chamber 151–2

Statutory Returns 25
Supreme Court of Justice 152
Syrett, D. 125

Tamblin, Stuart 143
taxation records 67, 139–40, 167–70, 186–8, 217–20
Taylor, N. 215
Thomas, G. 128
Thomas, M.J. 47
The Times Digital Archive 208
topographical maps 6, 36
tradesmen 162–3, 184
training colleges 64–6
transportation 139, 144–5
Treasury class 168

universities 64

Vicar General 100–1
The Victoria Histories of the Counties of England 63, 164–5
vocational training 66–8

Wallis, P.J. and R.V. 182
Watts, M.J. and C. 119
Webb, Cliff 70, 156
Whitmore, J.B. 209
wills 209–17, 220
Wilson, E. 123
Wise, T. and S. 113
Wolfson, Patricia 200
workhouse records 49, 155; see also Overseers of the Poor
World War I 119–22

Yeo, Geoffrey 28, 90
yeomanry 128–9